Health Science Projects About

Anatomy and Physiology

Other titles in the **Science Projects** *series*

Health Science Projects About

Anatomy and Physiology

Robert Gardner

Science Projects

Enslow Publishers, Inc.

40 Industrial Road   PO Box 38
Box 398   Aldershot
Berkeley Heights, NJ 07922   Hants GU12 6BP
USA   UK
http://www.enslow.com

Library of Congress Cataloging-in-Publication Data

Gardner, Robert, 1929–
  Health science projects about anatomy and physiology/ Robert Gardner.
      p. cm. — (Science projects)
Includes bibliographical references and index.
  ISBN 0-7660-1440-1
  1. Human physiology—Juvenile literature 2. Biology projects—Juvenile literature.
[1. Body, Human—Experiments. 2. Human physiology—Experiments. 3. Experiments.
4. Science projects.] I. Title
  QP37 .G359 2001
  612'.0078—dc21

                                                            00-011745

Printed in the United States of America

10 9 8 7 6 5 4 3 2

To Our Readers: We have done our best to make sure all Internet addresses in this book
were active and appropriate when we went to press. However, the author and the publisher
have no control over and assume no liability for the material available on those Internet sites
or on other Web sites they may link to. Any comments or suggestions can be sent by e-mail
to comments@enslow.com or to the address on the back cover.

Illustration Credits: Stephen F. Delisle, pp. 14, 27, 41, 43, 50, 58, 70, 77, 79, 98,
103; Enslow Publishers, Inc., pp. 21, 54(a), 106; Jacob Katari, p. 74; LifeArt image
copyright 1998 Lippincott Williams & Wilkins. All rights reserved, pp. 12, 16, 19,
23, 34, 35, 36, 45(b), 54(b), 68, 82, 84, 86, 93, 100.

Cover Illustration: Jerry McCrea (foreground); © Corel Corporation
(background).

Contents

*appropriate ideas for science fair project

Illustrations

*appropriate ideas for science fair project

Introduction

The science projects and experiments in this book involve human anatomy and physiology. Anatomy has to do with the structure of the body: the way it is put together. Physiology is concerned with the way the body functions. These two subjects are closely related because it is difficult to understand how the body works without knowing how it is put together.

For some of the experiments you will need friends or family members who are willing to serve as subjects. You will also need people to help you with experiments that require more than one pair of hands. Since some of the experiments will take some time, try to choose friends who are patient. It might be best if you work with people who enjoy experimenting as much as you do. In that way you could take turns being experimenter and subject.

As you do these projects, you will find it useful to record your ideas, notes, data, and anything you can conclude from your experiments in a notebook. In that way you can keep track of the information you gather and the conclusions you reach. It will allow you to refer to experiments you have already done that may be useful in later projects.

Missing Topics?

Some topics—such as the senses (sight, hearing, touch, taste, and smell), food and nutrition, and reproduction—that you might expect to find in a book on anatomy and physiology are not covered in this book. Another book in this series—*Health Science Projects About Your Senses*—is devoted entirely to the senses. Still another book in the series—*Health Science Projects About Nutrition*—is a rich source of experiments related to food and nutrition. Finally, there are so many books about the human life cycle, reproduction, and related issues that a chapter devoted to the subject would be superfluous.

Science Fairs

Some of the projects in this book might be appropriate for a science fair. Those projects are indicated with an asterisk (*). However, judges at such fairs do not reward projects or experiments that are simply copied from a book. For example, a model of the human eye, which is commonly found at these fairs, would probably not impress judges unless it was done in a novel or creative way. A model of the eye with a flexible lens that could produce images of objects at any distance from the eye would receive more consideration than a rigid papier-mâché model.

Science fair judges tend to reward creative thought and imagination. However, it is difficult to be creative or imaginative unless you are really interested in your project, so choose something that appeals to you. Consider, too, your own ability and the cost of materials needed for the project.

If you decide to use a project found in this book for a science fair, you will need to find ways to modify or extend the project. This should not be difficult, because you will probably find that as you do these projects new ideas for experiments will come to mind. These new experiments could make excellent science fair projects, particularly because they spring from your own thoughts and are interesting to you.

If you decide to enter a science fair and have never done so before, you should read some of the books listed in the Further Reading section on page 123. The references that deal specifically with science fairs will provide plenty of helpful hints and lots of useful information that will enable you to avoid the pitfalls that sometimes plague first-time entrants. You will learn how to prepare appealing reports that include charts and graphs, how to set up and display your work, how to present your project, and how to relate to judges and visitors.

Safety First

Most of the projects included in this book are perfectly safe. However, the following safety rules are well worth reading before you start any project.

1. Do any experiments or projects, whether from this book or of your own design, under the supervision of a science teacher or other knowledgeable adult.

2. Read all instructions carefully before proceeding with a project. If you have questions, check with your supervisor before going any further.

3. Maintain a serious attitude while conducting experiments. Fooling around can be dangerous to you and to others.

4. Wear approved safety goggles when you are doing anything that might cause injury to your eyes.

5. Do not eat or drink while experimenting.

6. Have a first-aid kit nearby while you are experimenting.

7. Do not put your fingers or any object in electrical outlets.

8. Never experiment with household electricity except under the supervision of a knowledgeable adult.

9. Never touch a lit high-wattage bulb. Lightbulbs produce light, but they also produce heat.

10. Never look directly at the sun. It can cause permanent damage to your eyes.

11. Many substances are poisonous. Do not taste them unless instructed to do so.

12. Avoid wearing loose clothing while you do experiments. It might get caught in equipment or a flame, or knock over and possibly break equipment.

1

Your Skin, Skeleton, and Joints

The human body is made up of nearly a hundred trillion (100,000,000,000,000) cells. The cells are of 100 different types, clustered into five kinds of tissue: muscle, nerve, blood, connective (which supports or covers organs), and epithelial (which covers or lines other tissues).

Your skin is a protective cover of epidermal cells (epithelial tissue) that blankets a layer of connective tissue known as the dermis. Dermis cells anchor the skin to underlying connective tissue, muscles, and bones. Within the dermis are blood vessels, nerve cells, sweat glands, and hair follicles. (See Figure 1.) Fingernails, toenails, and hair grow out of the skin.

Your skin provides protection from infection, drying out, harmful rays, and injury. It is essential in regulating body temperature, and it contains a variety of sensory organs that respond to touch, pressure, temperature, and pain. Because water and salts are lost through the skin, it also serves a role in excreting body wastes.

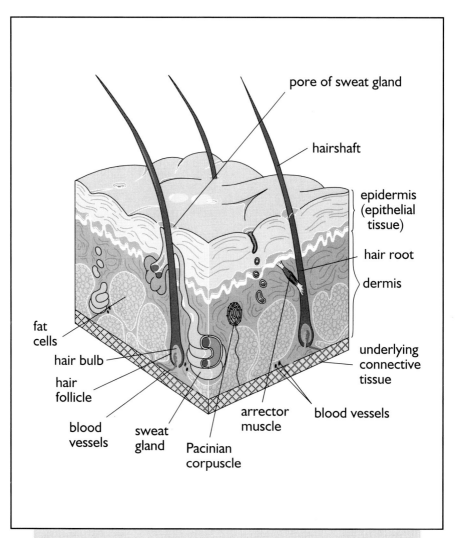

pore of sweat gland

hairshaft

epidermis
(epithelial
tissue)

hair root

dermis

underlying
connective
tissue

blood vessels

fat
cells

hair bulb

hair
follicle

blood
vessels

sweat
gland

Pacinian
corpuscle

arrector
muscle

Figure 1. A small section of skin greatly magnified. The Pacinian corpuscle
responds to pressure by generating nerve impulses.

1-1*
Your Skin: Wet and Dry

As you know, exercise can make you sweat. To see how sweat helps to regulate your body temperature, use an eyedropper to place a few drops of alcohol and an equal number of water drops on a piece of waxed paper. Which liquid disappears (evaporates) first?

Things you will need:
- eyedropper
- alcohol
- water
- waxed paper
- socks
- fan

Now place the same number of drops of each liquid on your forearm. Spread the drops out over your skin. Which liquid makes your skin feel cooler?

On a warm, dry (not humid) day, put a dry sock on one foot and a sock you have dipped in warm water on the other. After several minutes, which foot feels cooler? Can you explain why it feels cooler? Do you detect any change if you place both feet in front of a fan?

Exploring on Your Own

Design and carry out an experiment to see how temperature affects the rate at which water evaporates.

The skin on your fingertips has friction ridges. If you look closely, you can see them. Design a technique to record fingerprints. Then collect fingerprints from a number of people. Can you find any two sets of fingerprints that are the same?

How do detectives lift fingerprints from a surface?

Investigate the use of fingerprints in forensic science.

1-2
How Fast Do Fingernails Grow?

Fingernails, like hair, are appendages of your skin. You know that fingernails grow—you have to keep cutting them—but how fast?

Things you will need:

- nail file
- ruler
- several people of different genders and ages

To find out, use the edge of a nail file to make a short straight line across the base of your thumbnail within the white, semicircular cuticle, as seen in Figure 2. Measure the distance from the file mark to the inside edge of the white band at the end of your nail. A week later make the same measurement. The difference between the two measurements will tell you how much your nail grew in one week.

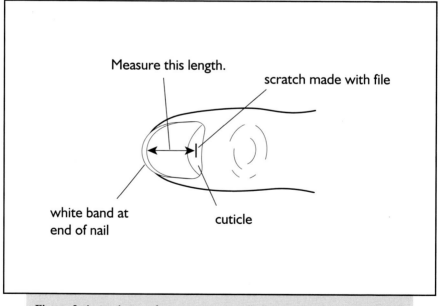

Measure this length.

scratch made with file

white band at end of nail

cuticle

Figure 2. A simple set of measurements will allow you to find out how fast your fingernails grow. What will happen to the distance between the scratch and the white band at the end of the nail as time passes?

Continue measuring your thumbnail's growth each week. Does your thumbnail grow at a constant speed? What is the rate of the nail's growth in millimeters or inches per month? How much would it grow in a year? Which is growing faster, your nail or your height? Do your other fingernails and toenails grow faster or slower than your thumbnail?

Measure the fingernail growth rate of a number of people. Do the nails of females grow faster than those of males? Is the growth rate affected by age? Do nails grow faster in the summer than in the winter? If they do, how can you find out whether it is related to temperature, hours of daylight per day, or some other factor, such as nutrition?

Your Skeleton

A house has a hidden frame to which everything else is attached. Your body is similar. Beneath your skin and flesh lies the frame— the bony skeleton—to which your body is attached. Although the bones of an adult weigh only about 9 kilograms (20 pounds), they provide a sound framework because they are stronger than reinforced concrete.

Bones are more than a frame, they enclose and protect your brain, spinal cord, and other organs. The marrow inside bones produces the red blood cells that carry oxygen and the white blood cells that help you combat infections.

You were born with more than 300 separate bones. By the time you are an adult, that number will be just a few more than 200, because many of the separate bones fuse together.

Figure 3a is a frontal view of the major bones that make up an adult skeleton. Figure 3b is a rear view of that skeleton.

The skeleton is divided into two parts. The axial skeleton consists of the skull, vertebrae (backbone), ribs, and sternum. The bones attached to the axial skeleton—the arms, legs, scapula, clavicle, and pelvis—constitute the appendicular skeleton.

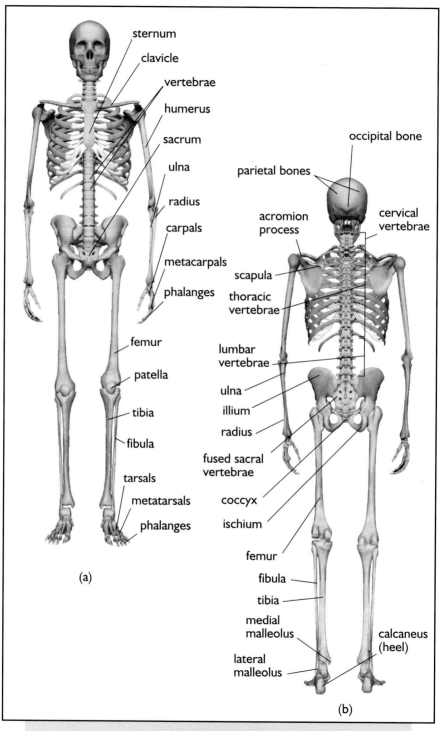

Figure 3. The human skeleton as seen from the a) front and b) back.

Bones are held together and connected by ligaments. Muscles, which are connected to your bones by tendons, enable you to move some of your bones. The points about which your bones move relative to one another are called joints.

1-3*
Locating Parts of Your Skeleton

You cannot see the bones in your body. They are covered with muscles, connective tissue, and skin. The common names of the body regions covering your bones are shown in Figure 4.

Things you will need:

• a partner, preferably one who is thin so you can easily feel his or her bones

Even though you cannot see your bones, you can feel many of them. Your skull, for example, feels like one large bone. It is actually a number of separate bones that have fused or are fusing (see Figure 5). The gaps that existed between your skull bones when you were a baby allowed your brain to grow. That is necessary because

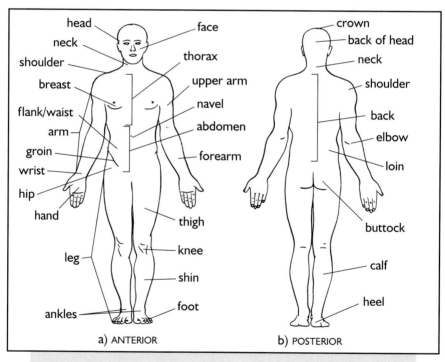

Figure 4. The common names for the various regions of your body. a) Anterior view. b) Posterior view.

18

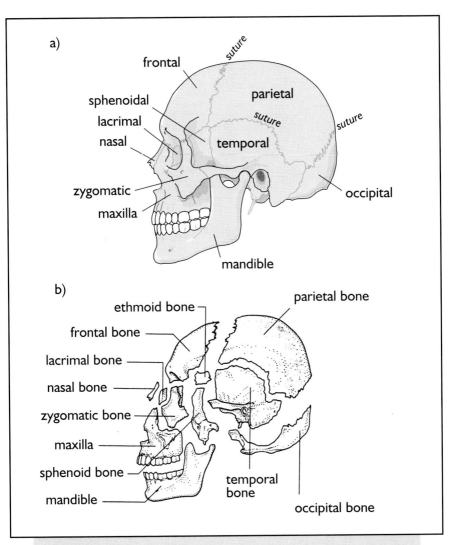

a)

frontal
suture
sphenoidal
parietal
lacrimal
suture
suture
nasal
temporal
zygomatic
occipital
maxilla

mandible

b)

parietal bone
ethmoid bone
frontal bone
lacrimal bone
nasal bone
zygomatic bone
maxilla
sphenoid bone
temporal bone
mandible
occipital bone

Figure 5. The human skull showing a) side view and b) individual bones that make up the skull.

at birth human brains are only one-third their adult size. During its first year, the average baby's brain grows from 400 g (14 oz) to 990 g (35 oz). By age 6 or 7, a child's brain is fully grown (1300 g or 46 oz), which is why a child's head appears to be too large for its body.

The three bones of the middle ear (hammer, anvil, and stirrup) move when the eardrum vibrates. The only other bone in your head that moves is your mandible, or lower jaw. It moves when you talk or chew. Your lower teeth are embedded in your mandible. The front part of the mandible constitutes your chin.

Mandible

Beginning at your chin, feel back along one side of your mandible. You will find that the rear end of the mandible turns upward at almost a right angle to articulate (form a joint) with the rest of the skull. The bone is connected to other bones of the head by ligaments. Tendons connect the mandible to muscles that make it move.

Clavicle, Sternum, and Scapula

At the base of your neck, on either side, you can feel the clavicle (collarbone). You will find that it extends laterally (sideways) on both sides. Near the center of your upper chest it connects with your sternum. You can feel the outer side of the sternum (breastbone). It runs down the center of your chest toward your abdomen. It narrows at its lower end to form a slightly pointed structure known as the xiphoid process. The outer end of your clavicle connects with the scapula (shoulder blade).

Feel a friend's scapula. It has a ridge, called the spine, that ends at the acromion process. It is the part of the shoulder farthest from the middle of the body. Below the acromion process is a concave depression known as the glenoid cavity.

Arm, Wrist, and Hand

The rounded end of the humerus (upper arm bone) fits into and can rotate in the glenoid cavity. You can feel the shaft of your humerus at the center of your upper arm. But the upper end lies under the acromion process and muscle tissue. You will find that the lower end of the humerus is wide and articulates with the two bones of the lower arm.

What we normally call the elbow, or funny bone, is the upper end of the ulna. If you follow the ulna downward, you will find that it ends in the knobby styloid process above the little-finger side of the wrist.

The styloid process of the other bone of the lower arm—the radius—can be found above the thumb side of the wrist. You can follow the radius upward to the point where it articulates with the humerus.

The wrist is made up of eight small bones called the carpals, which are difficult to identify individually. You can, however, feel the five metacarpal bones on the back of your hand. The lower ends of these bones articulate with the phalanges, or fingers. There are a total of fourteen phalanges on each hand. Three are found in each finger and two in the thumb. The joints where metacarpals and phalanges meet are commonly known as your knuckles.

As you can see in Figure 6, many mammals have the same arm bones, even though their relative sizes and functions vary greatly. Such structures are said to be homologous: the bones have the same origin and basic structure even though they serve different purposes.

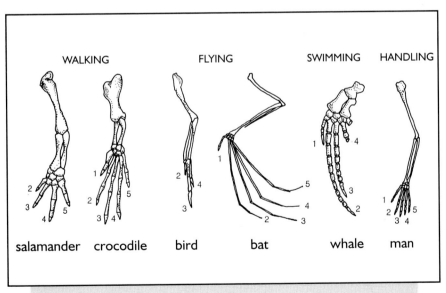

Figure 6. These forelimbs are homologous. What differences do you see? What do the numbers indicate?

Back and Ribs

The skull sits atop the thirty-three bones that make up the vertebral column. There are seven cervical vertebrae in the neck, twelve thoracic vertebrae at the rear of the chest, and five lumbar vertebrae in the lower back. By adulthood, the five sacral vertebrae and four coccygeal vertebrae fuse with one another and with the pelvis. The fused sacral vertebrae are referred to as the sacrum. The fused coccygeal vertebrae are called the *coccyx*. In many animals the coccygeal vertebrae are separate and more numerous. They are the bones that lie within an animal's tail.

The vertebral column encloses and protects the spinal cord—the body's major nerve cells that connect the brain with the muscles and sensory cells of the body below the head. Many of the vertebrae have spinal processes that you can feel if you run your fingers along a friend's backbone. The thoracic vertebrae also have transverse processes that articulate with the twelve ribs on each side of the body, which you can also feel.

The ribs surround the lungs and heart, which lie within the upper body's thoracic cavity. You can trace the path of one or more of the ribs from a thoracic vertebrae on the back to the sternum at the front of the body. The lower two ribs are called floating ribs. They do not attach to the sternum. The three pairs of ribs above the floaters join together to form a common band of cartilage that attaches to the sternum beside the xiphoid process. The remaining seven pairs of ribs end in cartilage that connect them directly to the sternum. At least part of each of these upper seven pairs of ribs lies under the scapula, so it is difficult to trace these ribs all the way from vertebra to sternum.

Pelvis, Legs, and Feet

The pelvis, shown in Figure 7, is similar in some ways to the shoulders. Just as the arms articulate with the shoulder bones, so the legs articulate with the pelvis. The rear of the pelvis is fused with the sacral and coccygeal vertebrae. It feels like a solid plate that covers the lower part of the back. The sides of the pelvis are formed by the ilium bones (hipbones) that you can feel on either side of your belly. The bottom of the pelvis consists of the ischium bones, the bones you sit on. The pubis bones form the front of the pelvis. They join to form the pubic symphysis at the middle of the very lowest part of your abdomen. You can feel them on either side of your body at the base of your groin.

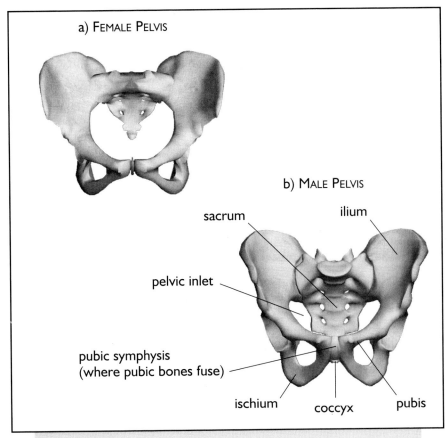

Figure 7. The female pelvis (a) is wider and shallower than the male pelvis (b). Both, however, have the same bones. They are simply slightly different in shape.

The femur (upper leg bone) is the longest bone in your body. The rounded head at its upper end fits into a concavity in the pubis. You can feel the outer upper end of the femur move as you walk. Feel, too, the very wide lower end of your femur. It lies behind your patella (kneecap).

The lower end of the femur articulates with the tibia (shinbone), the larger of the two bones of the lower leg. You can feel the entire front side of the tibia. Start just below the patella and follow it to its bulblike end on the inner (medial) side of your leg beside the ankle. The bulblike end of the tibia, the medial malleolus, has its complement on the other side of the ankle—the lateral malleolus. However, the lateral malleolus is the lower end of the fibula, which lies on the outer (lateral) side of your leg. How far can you trace the fibula up your leg?

Like the wrist, the ankle consists of a number of bones—the tarsals, of which there are seven. The largest tarsal bone is the heel bone or calcaneus, which you can feel on the lower rear portion of your foot.

The metatarsals lie between the toes and the ankle and correspond to the metacarpals in the hand. You can probably feel all five of your metatarsals by moving your fingers over the top of your foot behind your toes.

The front ends of the metatarsals articulate with the phalanges, commonly known as toes. Each foot, like your hands, has a total of fourteen phalanges. There are three phalanges in each of the four smaller toes and two in the great (big) toe.

You have now examined as many of the bones from your head to your toes as you can feel. Which bones were you not able to feel?

Exploring on Your Own

On a real or plastic model of a human skeleton, or on detailed anatomical diagrams, identify all of the bones found in a human adult.

What are the meanings of the words *axial* and *appendicular* as they apply to your skeleton?

Police often ask anthropologists to examine skeletal remains at crime scenes. Why do police ask anthropologists to examine skeletons? How do anthropologists distinguish between male and female skeletons?

Visit a science museum where the skeletons of different animals are on display. Can you identify bones similar to those found in humans in the bodies of these other animals?

Broken bones—fractures—are common injuries. What are the various types of fractures and how are they treated?

1-4*
Joints: Where Bones Meet

The places where different bones articulate are called joints. Having examined the various bones of your body, you know that not all joints are the same.

Things you will need:

• a partner, preferably one who is thin so you can readily feel his or her bones

• 3 soda straws

• scissors

• string

Fixed Joints

Some of your joints are fixed. They do not allow movement. The bones of your skull, which were separate and distinct at birth, become fused with time. The lines along which they join are known as sutures. Fixed joints are also found in many bones of the face.

Slightly Movable Joints

The ends of bones that have limited movement at a joint are generally padded with cartilage or joined by slightly flexible ligaments. The lower ends of the tibia and fibula are joined by such ligaments so that these two bones may undergo slight movement with respect to one another.

The cartilage between the bones of the pelvis allows slight movement. Between the vertebrae that make up your backbone, there are disks of cartilage that permit twisting, compression, and extension. The movement between adjacent vertebrae is limited. However, because there are many vertebrae, your back has considerable flexibility. Through approximately what angle can you bend your back forward? Backward?

To see how many vertebrae make flexibility possible even though movement between any two is limited, try this experiment. Take two soda straws. Cut one straw into 10 or 12 pieces. Leave the other straw whole. Run a length of string through each straw.

Hold the ends of each straw as shown in Figure 8. Which straw provides greater flexibility?

To see why it is advantageous to have many vertebrae, cut a third straw into three pieces and run a string through it. How does its flexibility compare with the straw that has ten or twelve segments?

Movable Joints

Most joints in your body are movable, but some provide a greater range of movement than others. The ends of bones in movable joints are covered by cartilage, and a membrane-enclosed fluid (synovial fluid) lies between them. The fluid serves as a lubricant for joints.

Pivot Joints

A pivot joint allows one bone to rotate on another in much the same way that a faucet turns. You can turn your head, as in shaking your

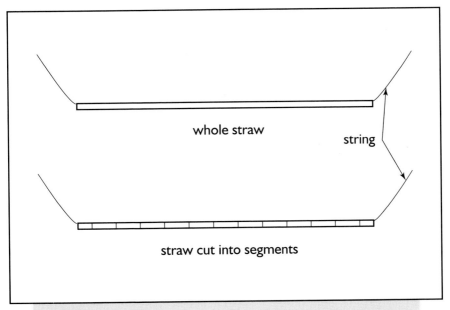

whole straw

string

straw cut into segments

Figure 8. A straw cut into many segments can serve as a model of the vertebrae that make up your backbone. The cut-up straw and the uncut one are both suspended on strings. How do the two compare with regard to flexibility?

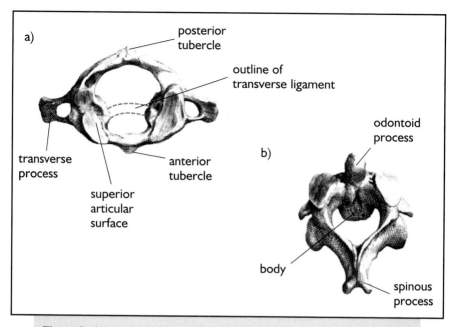

a)

posterior tubercle

outline of transverse ligament

odontoid process

transverse process

b)

anterior tubercle

superior articular surface

body

spinous process

Figure 9. a) A top view of the atlas, or first cervical vertebra (C-1). b) A side view of the axis, or second cervical vertebra (C-2). The odontoid process fits into the opening in front of the transverse ligament of the atlas. The atlas, which supports the skull's occipital bone, turns about the odontoid process.

head to indicate no, because of a pivot joint. The first two cervical vertebrae—the atlas (first) and the axis (second)—form this pivot joint. The long vertical process of the axis fits into an opening in the anterior (front) side of the atlas (see Figure 9). This allows the atlas, which is firmly attached to the head, to turn (pivot) right or left on the axis.

You can also turn your palm forward or backward by twisting your forearm because of another pivot joint. If your arm is very thin, you may be able to feel the radius turn as you turn your palm. The radius turns on a concave notch on the ulna on the inside of the elbow.

Hinge Joints

Hinge joints are so named because they allow bones to move in the same way that a door swings on its hinges. A door's hinge allows it to swing nearly 180 degrees, but no farther. Straighten your arm.

Then bend it slowly. Which bones move? Is the joint between your humerus and ulna a hinge joint? Why is the joint between your femur and tibia at your knee a hinge joint? Where else in your body can you find hinge joints?

Ball-and-Socket Joints

When the sphere-shaped end of one bone fits into a cuplike cavity in another bone, you have a ball-and-socket joint. Such a joint allows movement in many directions, and it allows rotation. The joint at your shoulder where the end of the humerus fits into the scapula's glenoid cavity provides you with your most mobile joint. In how many different directions can you move your upper arm? Can you rotate it in a complete circle?

Your other ball-and-socket joint is the articulation of your femur and pelvis. In how many directions can you move your upper leg? Why is it not as mobile as your shoulder joint?

Condyloid Joints

A condyloid joint is one in which the oval-shaped end (condyle) of one bone fits into the elliptical cavity of another. The radius and one of the carpal bones behind your thumb form a condyloid joint at your wrist. What kind of motion does this type of joint allow?

Saddle Joints

In a saddle joint, the two bones that articulate both have convex and concave surfaces that mesh. The only saddle joints in your body are the joints formed by the metacarpal bones behind your thumbs and one of the carpal bones in your wrist. Use one of your thumbs to find out what kind of motions a saddle joint allows.

Gliding Joints

A gliding joint, as its name implies, allows bones to glide over one another. Bones that meet in a gliding joint have nearly flat surfaces.

Such joints are found between carpal and tarsal bones and between vertebrae. Can you detect the motion of any gliding joints with your fingers?

Exploring on Your Own

What is the origin of the terms *atlas* and *axis* for the first two cervical vertebrae?

A person's weight while standing can squeeze joints together, particularly the vertebral joints. Could such squeezing change a person's height during the course of a day? Design and carry out an experiment to find out.

Often, when you bend your knees, raise your arm, or crack your knuckles, you hear a snapping sound. What causes such a sound?

People who can contort their limbs and phalanges well beyond the normal range of flexibility are often said to be double-jointed. Are they really double-jointed?

Life in a Jointless Body

Stand in the center of a room. Pretend that all your joints are frozen. You cannot bend your knees, arms, ankles, wrists, or even your fingers. Can you eat? Can you walk? Talk? Write? Turn your head? What can you do?

2

Muscles: The Prime Movers

All motions of your body, visible and invisible, are made possible by muscles. In addition to running, walking, and jumping, there are motions within your body that take place even when you are asleep. Your heart contracts about once every second throughout your life. You breathe because muscles move your ribs and diaphragm up and down. There are also muscles, of which you are totally unaware, that move food and fluids along your stomach and intestines or blood through your blood vessels. With so much to do, it is not surprising that muscles account for nearly half your weight.

All muscle tissue possesses irritability, contractility, extensibility, and elasticity. *Irritability* means that a muscle will respond to nerve impulses. *Contractility* is its ability to contract, to become shorter and thicker. Such contraction can cause a bone to move. *Extensibility* means that muscle tissue can be stretched or extended by a force. *Elasticity* means that a muscle, like a rubber band, resumes its original size after being extended.

Muscles are made up of many elongated cells known as fibers that are held together by connective tissue. There are three types of muscle tissue. Striated muscle, when viewed through a microscope, has stripes across its cells. It is the type of muscle that makes bones move. It is also called voluntary muscle because you can control its action. The biceps muscle on your upper arm is a striated or voluntary muscle. You decide voluntarily to contract that muscle and thereby lift your forearm. Nonstriated or smooth muscles are also known as involuntary muscles because you cannot control, nor are you consciously aware of, their action. You may, however, hear the results of their contraction. The gurgling sounds in your abdomen are the result of smooth muscle contractions around your stomach and intestines that cause fluids to move.

The third type of muscle—cardiac muscle—is found only in the heart. Its fibers have striations, but they are less distinct than in skeletal muscle, and the cells are smaller. The heart acts as one large muscle. When it contracts, it squeezes blood from the heart into two major arteries that lead to all parts of the body.

In experiments involving single muscle fibers, scientists use an electric current as a stimulus. The results of such experiments show that when the current reaches sufficient strength (minimal stimulus), the fiber will contract its maximum amount. Increasing the strength of the stimulus has no effect on the contraction, and any stimulus less than minimal will have no effect. This is known as the all-or-none law. Each muscle cell gives its maximum response or none at all.

In an ordinary muscle contraction, many fibers are stimulated. The total force exerted by the muscle depends on the number of fibers that contract. If you use a muscle to raise the maximum load it can lift, all the fibers in the muscle will contract. In most muscle activity, only a fraction of the fibers contract at any one time. To avoid fatigue, some fibers will contract while others relax.

2-1*
Your Muscles

No materials needed

With more than 600 skeletal muscles in your body, you can move your body in many ways. A skeletal muscle generally has its origin (attachment of one end) on one bone that remains relatively fixed. Its other end—its insertion—is attached to the bone that moves when the muscle contracts. Both attachments, whether origin or insertion, are made by fibrous tendons that connect muscle to bone.

In this experiment, you will feel and identify some of your muscles. You will find Figure 10 useful as you search for muscles. Perhaps the muscle most familiar to you is your biceps or, more properly, your biceps brachii. It is the muscle on your arm that you show when someone says, "Make a muscle." The *biceps* part of the name means that the muscle has two heads and two origins. The *brachii* part of the name is from the Latin word *bracchium*, which means "arm."

Both origins of the biceps brachii are on the shoulder. The insertion of this muscle is found at the upper end of the radius. Place your hand on your biceps as you make a muscle by contracting it. As the muscle shortens, two things happen. The radius is lifted (and with it the lower arm). At the same time, the radius is turned outward so that the palm of your hand is turned upward.

You can use another muscle—the brachialis—to bend your arm. The brachialis lies under the biceps. Its origin is on the humerus. Its insertion is on the ulna. Bend your arm again, but this time keep your palm turned downward so that the radius does not turn about the ulna. As you can feel, the biceps does not contract. It is pushed up a little by the contracting brachialis muscle, but the upper arm feels much more flaccid than it did before. Now turn the palm over. You will immediately feel the biceps pop up.

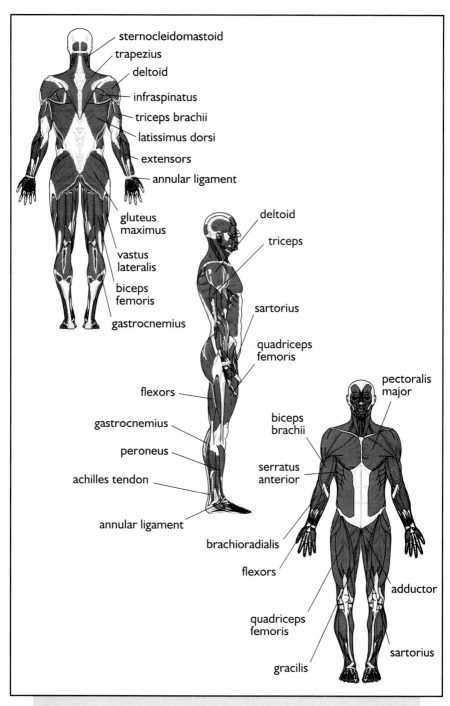

Figure 10. The major muscles of the body as seen from the back, side, and front.

If a bone can be moved to a certain position, it can be returned to where it was previously. Muscles are paired so that movements can be reversed. Just as you can flex (bend) your arm by contracting your biceps or brachialis muscles, so you can use a muscle to extend (straighten) the arm. The muscle that straightens your arm is the triceps brachii. What can you tell about this muscle just from its name?

Place your hand on the back of your upper arm when your arm is flexed. Can you feel the triceps contract as you fully straighten your arm? What can you assume about the location of the triceps' insertion? Where might its origin(s) be located?

The large muscles that cover your shoulder joints and make them appear round are the deltoids (Figures 10 and 11). Their origins are on the clavicle, acromion process, and scapula. Their

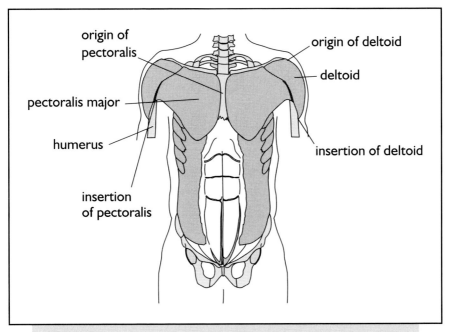

Figure 11. These muscles have opposing effects on the motion of the humerus. The deltoids (there is also one in the rear that has its origin on the scapula) lift the humerus. The pectoralis lowers the humerus.

insertions are on the outside of the humerus bones. Can you predict what will happen when one of your deltoid muscles contracts? Try it. Were you right?

The pectoralis major opposes the action of the deltoid on the same side of the body. Place your hand on the upper side of your chest. You can feel pectoralis major contract as you pull your arm downward and move it across your chest. Explain how the origins and insertions of pectoralis major make this movement possible (see Figure 11).

The muscle that extends your fingers is the extensor digitorum communis (Figure 12a). It can be felt the on the upper side of your lower arm when you extend your fingers. At the same time, beneath the skin on the back of your hand you can see the movement of the tendons that connect the muscle to the fingers. Extending your index finger alone will enable you to see a single tendon moving beneath the skin.

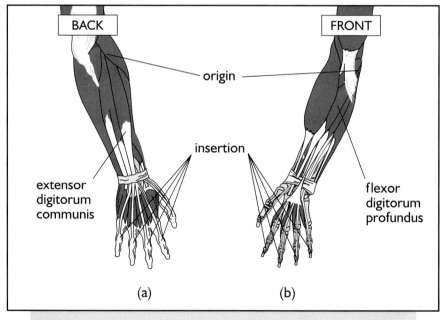

Figure 12. Opposing muscles extend (a) and flex (b) the fingers of the right hand.

Figure 12b shows the flexor digitorum profundus, which you use to bend your fingers. Place your fingers on the inside of your opposite forearm and feel this muscle contract. At the same time, you can see the tendons that connect this muscle to the fingers moving beneath the skin on your forearm. Can you find the muscles that extend and flex your thumbs? Can you see the movement of the tendons that connect these muscles to the thumbs?

Exploring on Your Own

Find the muscles and tendons used to flex and extend your knee joint. Then find the muscles used to flex and extend your foot. Use an anatomy book to find the names as well as the origins and insertions of these muscles.

What is the advantage of having the muscles that control the fingers and thumbs located so far from the hands?

The gastrocnemius and soleus muscles in your calf are connected to your heel bone by the Achilles tendon. It is the strongest and thickest tendon in your body. You can find the story of Achilles in a book on Greek mythology. After reading the story, explain why this tendon was named for him.

2-2
Muscle Pairs

Muscles can only contract; they cannot expand. As a result, muscles pull. They do not push. Therefore, if a muscle or muscle group bends a joint, there must be another muscle or muscle group to pull it the opposite way to straighten the joint.

Things you will need:

• spring-type bathroom scale
• chair
• wall
• partner

In many muscle pairs, one muscle is stronger than the other. You can use a spring-type bathroom scale to compare the strengths of muscle pairs. Consider the muscles that allow you to kick both forward and backward. Are they of equal strength?

To find out, sit on a chair facing a wall. Place the scale upright against the wall. With what force can you push your foot forward against the scale? Now place the scale between your leg and the leg of the chair. With what force can you push backward with your heel? You may need a partner to read the scale while you are pushing.

Figure out ways to place the scale so you can compare the strengths of other muscle pairs. How does the strength of the biceps and brachialis muscles that bend your arm compare with the strength of the triceps muscle that straightens your arm?

Compare the strengths of the muscles in the pairs used to (1) turn your toes upward or downward; (2) squeeze your fingers into a fist or open them; (3) move your head forward or backward; (4) move your upper arm forward or backward; (5) bend or straighten your leg at the knee.

2-3*
Muscle Fatigue

Pick up the bathroom scale you used in the previous experiment and hold it in your hands.

Squeeze the scale as tightly as you can with your hands. What is the maximum squeeze force you can exert on the scale with your hands?

Next, open and close your hands to make and open a fist as fast as you can for a minute or until you cannot do it anymore. Then squeeze the scale again. How strong are your hands now? How can you explain the difference in hand strength?

Exploring on Your Own

As you have seen, fatigue affects the short-term strength of a muscle. Does it also affect your ability to control the muscle? Design an experiment to find out.

2-4
Your Opposable Thumb

Although walking on two legs creates stresses that can result in lower back pain, torn knee or pelvic cartilages, varicose veins, hernias, or fallen arches, it does free our hands to perform those tasks that distinguish us from other animals. We can use our hands to carry food, to make and use tools, and to write—a means of communication unknown to other animals.

Things you will need:

• a partner

• tape

Our hands are not only free, but they have opposable thumbs. You will find that you can touch the tips of any of your other fingers with your thumb. To see the significance of an anatomy that provides an opposable thumb, have someone tape your thumbs to your palms so that you cannot use them.

What tasks do you now find difficult or impossible?

2-5
Your Always Active Muscles

To avoid fatigue, your muscle fibers do not usually all contract at the same time. While some are contracting, others are in a relaxed state. As the contracted muscle fibers approach fatigue,

Things you will need:

• paper clip
• table knife
• table or countertop

their job is taken over by fibers that were previously relaxed. As a result, your muscle fibers are constantly sharing the workload. Evidence of this can be found by doing a simple experiment.

Partially open a paper clip and hang it on the end of a table knife, as shown in Figure 13. Hold the tip of the paper clip as close as possible to a table or countertop without touching it. You will hear the tip of the paper clip occasionally touching the table. Why are you unable to hold the paper clip perfectly still?

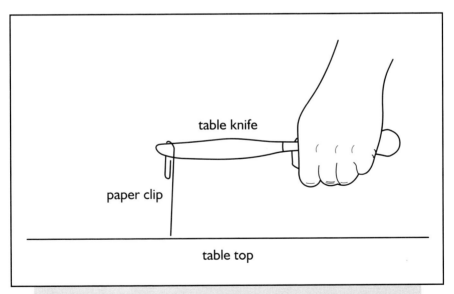

Figure 13. Why can't you keep a paper clip perfectly still when it is hanging from the end of a knife that you hold in your hand?

Try this same experiment after exercising. Open and close your hands as fast as you can for a minute or until you cannot do it anymore. Then try to hold the paper clip perfectly still at the end of the knife. Does exercise affect your ability to control your muscles? If it does, how, and how can you explain it?

Muscles and Levers

In the human body, muscles and bones act together as levers. A simple lever is a rigid rod that is free to move about a fixed point of support called the fulcrum. When in use, two forces act on the lever at different points. One force, the resistance force, may be regarded as something to be lifted or balanced. The second force, the effort force, is exerted to overcome or balance the resistance force.

In Figure 14a, the resistance force is the weight of the rock. A worker exerts a force (the effort force) at the other end of the lever in order to lift the rock. The rock, which is 25 cm (0.25 m) from the fulcrum, weighs 100 kg. To lift the rock, the worker, who is exerting a force 100 cm (1.0 m) from the fulcrum, must push down on the lever with a force of at least 25 kg. We can predict the force needed because of a scientific law based on experiments. This law tells us that for the resistance force to be balanced by the effort force, E x D must be equal to R x d. E is the effort force and D is the distance of the effort force from the fulcrum. R is the resistance force and d is the distance of the resistance force from the fulcrum. For the example shown in Figure 14a, 100 kg x 0.25 m = 25 kg x 1.0 m.

There are three classes of levers based on the relative position of fulcrum, effort, and resistance. With first-class levers (Figure 14a), the fulcrum lies between the resistance and the effort. As a result, the resistance or load moves in the opposite direction from the effort.

In second-class levers, the resistance lies between the fulcrum and the effort; consequently, the resistance moves in the same direction

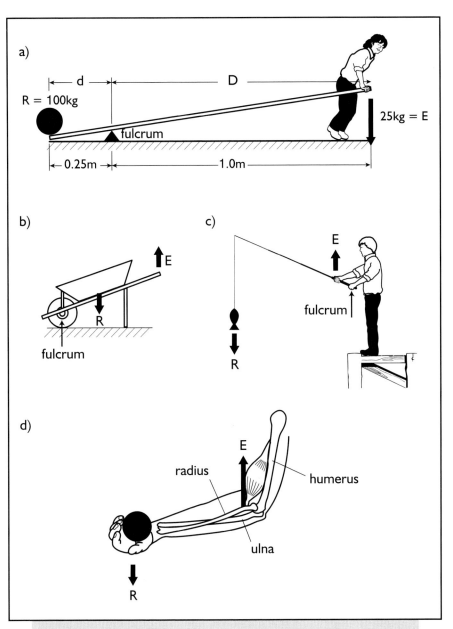

Figure 14. a) For the loads on a lever to balance, R x d must equal E x D. In the case shown, 100 kg x 0.25 m = 25 kg x 1.0 m. The lever shown is a first-class lever. b) a wheelbarrow is an example of a second-class lever. c) A fishing pole is an example of a third-class lever. d) The forearm and muscles on the upper arm constitute a lever system. What class lever is this system?

as the effort. A wheelbarrow (Figure 14b) is an example of a second-class lever.

In third-class levers, such as a fishing pole (Figure 14c), the effort lies between the fulcrum and the resistance. Since the distance from fulcrum to resistance is greater than from fulcrum to effort, the effort force must be greater than the resistance force.

2-6*
Muscles and Body Levers

There are many muscles and **No materials needed** bones acting as levers in your body. Put your chin on your chest and your hand on the back of your neck. As you lift your head to its upright position, you can feel the capitis muscles (see Figure 15a) contracting to pull your head upward. The weight of your head can be considered to be at the center of your skull. The capitis muscles are inserted on the occipital bone at the back of your head. Which class of lever is this muscle-bone lever? The opposing muscle (Figure 15b) is the sternocleidomastoid, which pulls your head downward. Can you feel its

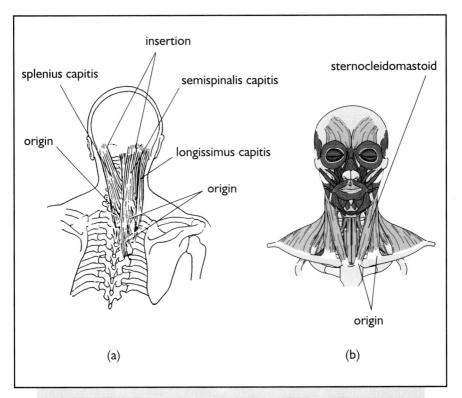

Figure 15. The muscles for a) extending and b) flexing the neck.

tendon on your clavicle when you pull your chin down onto your chest?

Hold a weight in your hand. Feel the tendon from the brachialis and biceps muscles as you bend your arm at the elbow and raise the weight. Look at Figure 14d, which shows how this lever works. What is the fulcrum for this muscle-bone lever? What class of lever is it? How will the effort force exerted by the muscle compare with the weight lifted in the hand?

What other muscle-bone levers can you find in your body? What is the class (first, second, or third) of each of the body levers you find? Do you find any second-class levers?

Exploring on Your Own

Design and build models to show how bones and muscles act as levers at various places in the body.

When you exercise, you use your muscles. What is the difference between

        a) isotonic and isometric exercises?

        b) aerobic and anaerobic exercises?

2-7
Seeing What's Under the Skin

You know that there are bones, muscles, tendons, and ligaments in your body. In this experiment you will actually see them by looking beneath the skin of an uncooked chicken wing that you can buy at a meat market. Put the chicken wing on a thick layer of newspapers. **Ask an adult to help you cut it apart** so that you can see the different tissues for yourself. The adult will need a sharp knife, and you will need a pair of tweezers, scissors, and a probe to pull and cut tissues, as well as soap and paper towels to wash your hands.

Things you will need:

• chicken wing

• newspapers

• an adult

• sharp knife

• tweezers

• scissors

• probe such as a skewer or finishing nail

• soap

• paper towels

• garbage container

Most of the skin covering the wing can be pulled away with your fingers. As you pull it off, look for connective tissue that attaches the skin to the muscles that lie under it.

The flesh beneath the skin and fatty layer is mostly muscle. Notice how each muscle is covered by a very thin transparent membrane. Use tweezers and a probe, such as a skewer or finishing nail, to separate the muscles from one another. See if you can find the origin and insertion of several of the muscles.

Find the tough, white, fibrous tendons that connect the muscles to bone. Use scissors to cut the tendons and remove the muscles to expose the bones. The major bones in the wing are very similar to your arm bones. Can you find the humerus? Can you find the radius and ulna? How do the carpals, metacarpals, and phalanges of a chicken differ from yours (see Figure 6)?

47

Find the wide, tough, white ligaments that connect the humerus to the radius and ulna. Use scissors to cut through the ligaments that join these bones. Examine the ends of the bones. Can you find glistening white cartilage covering the ends of the bones? What is the function of this cartilage? Can you find pads of yellow fat within the joint?

Ask the adult to cut away all the tissue along the bones. Place the tissue in a garbage container. Set the bones aside to dry in a warm, safe place. You will use them in the next experiment. **Wash your hands thoroughly with soap and water when you have finished handling the chicken wing.**

2-8*
Inside Bones

Place the dry humerus bone you saved from the previous experiment in a jar of vinegar. Does the bone sink or float? What does this tell you about the density of chicken bone? Do you think the bone of a seagull would be more or less dense than a chicken bone? What makes you think so?

Things you will need:
- bones from chicken wing
- jar
- vinegar
- newspapers
- an adult
- knife
- hacksaw
- two long beef or veal bones

Cover the jar and leave the other dry bones beside the jar. Vinegar is an acid. It will slowly dissolve the minerals in bone. These minerals constitute about two thirds of a bone's weight. Organic matter—bone and cartilage and blood vessel cells—make up the remaining third.

After several days, remove the bone from the jar. How does its flexibility compare with that of the dry bones you left beside the jar?

The soft, flexible, plasticlike material that remains after the minerals have been removed would eventually decay if buried in soil. Under proper conditions, the mineral or hard part of the whole bone would be preserved and form a fossil.

Place the bone that you have soaked in vinegar on some newspapers. **Ask an adult** to use a knife to cut the bone in half along its long axis to make what is called a longitudinal section. Then you can see what lies inside the bone. It will resemble the drawing in Figure 16, which shows a longitudinal section of a human long bone. The dense, or compact, bony tissue along the outside of the bone makes up the shaft of long bones. The spongy, or cancellous, bony tissue is found inside the shaft and especially near the ends of a bone. The medullary canal runs along the central shaft of a long

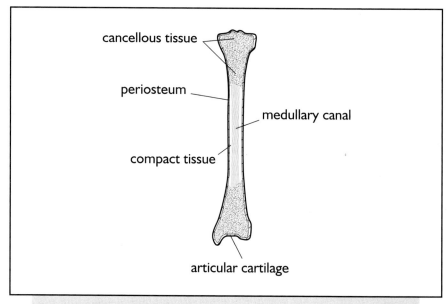

Figure 16. A longitudinal section of a human long bone.

bone. It contains yellow marrow, which is mostly fatty tissue, and blood vessels. Red marrow, which is found near the ends of long bones, contains cells known as erythroblasts. Erythroblasts produce red blood cells, the cells in your blood that transport oxygen. Except for their cartilaginous ends, bones are covered by a membrane called periosteum. The widened end of a long bone is called the epiphysis. The wider ends give the joints greater stability and serve to reduce the pressure on the bones.

Having seen the longitudinal section of a chicken bone, try to predict what the cross section will look like. Then **ask the adult** to cut across one of the *unsoftened* bones with a hacksaw. Does the cross section look the way you thought it would?

If possible, obtain two long beef or veal bones from a butcher. He or she might even cut one of them longitudinally for you. You can **ask the adult** to make several cuts across the other one when you reach home.

How do the longitudinal and cross sections of the beef bones compare with those of the chicken bones? Does the medullary canal of the beef bone extend all the way into the epiphysis?

Exploring on Your Own

Compare the densities of chicken and beef bones. Can you explain your results?

What minerals are found in bones? What foods must you eat to supply the minerals needed to make bone?

Paleontologists have found broken animal bones near the fossils of species believed to be the forerunners of today's humans. They believe the bones were broken to obtain the marrow that was inside. Why would these precursors of humans want bone marrow?

3

Circulation and Respiration

The process of respiration provides cells with the energy they need to live. The energy comes from the reaction between oxygen (obtained through respiration) and food. The reaction provides energy and releases carbon dioxide and water as waste products. In single-celled animals the oxygen and food simply diffuse across a cell membrane. The waste products leave the cell in the same way.

Humans have trillions of cells. Most of them are surrounded by other cells. The cells depend on blood to bring the food and oxygen they need and to carry away the waste products they produce. Blood circulates throughout the body inside blood vessels that lead to and from the heart. Arteries carry oxygen-rich blood from the heart, and veins carry the depleted blood back to the heart and then to the lungs. Between arteries and veins are capillaries—vessels with walls that are only one cell thick. It is through the walls of these tiny vessels that molecules of oxygen and food diffuse from the blood to the body cells. Similarly, waste products from the cells, such as carbon dioxide, diffuse into the blood through these same walls.

In your lungs, oxygen in the air you breathe diffuses into the blood. Carbon dioxide in your blood diffuses out into air that is exhaled from your lungs through your mouth and nose. The blood, which carries these gases to and from your lungs, is pumped to the lungs and to all the cells of your body by your heart.

You Have a Heart

Despite its association with such emotions and virtues as love and courage, the heart is basically a four-chambered pump. Figure 17a shows how the blood pumped from the heart circulates around the body. The blood vessels that contain blood rich in oxygen are shaded. Those that contain blood from which much of the oxygen has been removed are unshaded. The direction of blood flow is shown by the small arrows. A more detailed drawing of the heart itself is shown in Figure 17b.

Deoxygenated blood (blood that has lost much of its oxygen) is carried by several large veins to the heart's right atrium. The heart's contraction begins in the atria and forces blood into the ventricles. As contraction continues, deoxygenated blood in the right ventricle is pumped out of the heart into the pulmonary artery. This artery, which divides into right and left branches, transports blood to the lungs. These arteries divide further and eventually become capillaries, where the blood picks up oxygen from air inside the lungs. At the same time, it releases carbon dioxide to air in the lungs.

After being oxygenated, the blood enters the pulmonary veins and is carried to the heart's left atrium. Blood in this atrium is pumped into the left ventricle and from there out of the heart into the aorta—the body's major artery. The aorta divides into smaller arteries that bring blood to cells throughout the body. After giving up much of its oxygen in capillaries, blood returns to the heart's right atrium through veins.

The entire heart does not contract at the same time. A natural pacemaker, controlled by the vagus nerve from the brain, is located

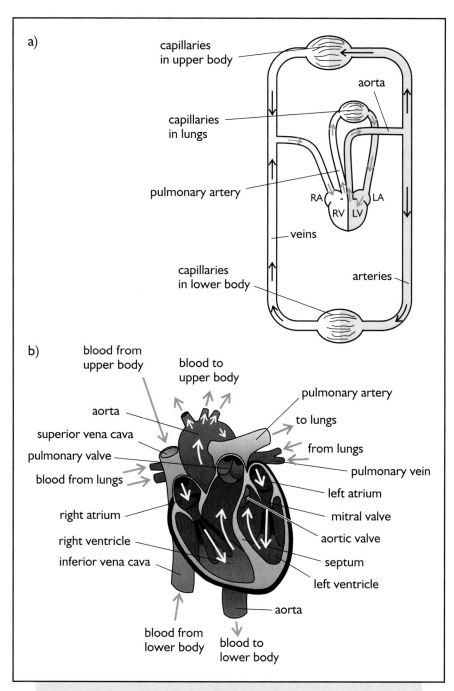

Figure 17. a) The general nature of the circulatory system. (R = right; L = left; A = atrium; V = ventricle) b) This is a more detailed look at the heart and the vessels leading to it (veins) and from it (arteries).

in the right atrium. It generates an electrical impulse that causes the heart to contract. The contraction begins in the atria, forcing blood in the atria through the bicuspid, or mitral valve, and tricuspid valve into the ventricles. When the impulse reaches the ventricles, they too contact. Their contraction slams shut the valves between the atria and ventricles and pushes blood out through the aortic and pulmonary valves into the aorta and pulmonary artery. After contracting, the heart relaxes and blood begins to pour into the atria from the body's major veins. At the same time, the blood pressure in the ventricles becomes less than in the aorta and pulmonary artery. This causes the aortic and pulmonary valves to close.

3-1*
Listening to a Heart

If you have access to a stethoscope, you can listen to your
own heart. Place the ear tips in
your ears and the chest piece
slightly to the left of the center
of your chest. Move the chest

Things you will need:

- stethoscope or a friend
- clock or watch
- rubber ball

piece slightly until you hear the heart sounds most clearly. Listen
for two sounds in close succession. The first is a relatively long
booming sound. The second is a short, sharp sound. Together they
sound like "lubb-dup." The *lubb* is caused by the contracting muscle and the closing of the valves between the ventricles and atria.
The *dup* is the sound of the aortic and pulmonary valves closing.

If you do not have a stethoscope, you can hear the same sounds
by placing your ear against the chest of a friend. Your friend will
probably want to hear your heart as well.

You have heard the heart of a body at rest. Do you think there
will be any change in the sounds after exercise?

To find out, run in place for five minutes. Or have your friend
run in place for the same length of time. Then listen to your heart
or his. Are the sounds the same or different? If they are different,
can you explain why they are different?

To have some understanding of how much work your heart does,
hold a rubber ball in your hand. The ball represents the blood that
must be squeezed out of the heart with each beat. Your hand represents the heart muscle that will do the squeezing. Squeeze the ball
at a steady rate of once every second.

How does your hand feel after several minutes? For your heart
to consistently pump blood every minute of your life, it needs
energy. That energy comes from the food carried to the muscle cells
of your heart by the blood. Why is it essential that the blood flow
to your heart not be obstructed or blocked?

Exploring on Your Own

What is an electrocardiograph and what is it used for? Examine an electrocardiogram. What is the significance of each part of the pattern? How does a cardiologist use an electrocardiogram to look for defects in a patient's heart?

What is lymph? What is the lymphatic system? What functions does it serve? What causes lymphatic fluid to move? From where and to where does it move?

3-2*
Finding a Pulse

With each contraction, your heart forces blood out into the arteries. The added blood swells the elastic walls of the large arteries near the heart, sending a pulse of expansion along the walls of all the arteries. You can feel this expansion of the radial artery in your wrist. Just place the first two fingers of one hand on the inside of your other wrist right behind your thumb, as shown in Figure 18a. Does each throb of your pulse reveal a beat of your heart?

Things you will need:
- a friend
- stethoscope
- table
- clay
- straw

To find out, place a stethoscope on a friend's chest and listen to his heart. While listening to his heart, place one hand on his pulse.

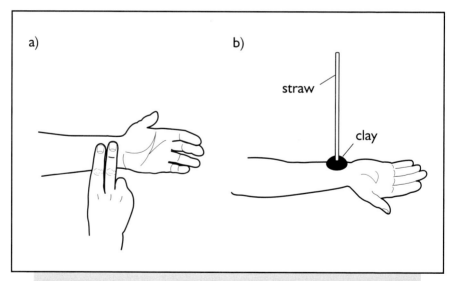

a)

b)

straw

clay

Figure 18. a) A pulse can be felt on the inside of your wrist just behind your thumb. b) You can use a lump of clay and a drinking straw to amplify your pulse and make it visible.

Does the pulse follow closely after the heartbeat? What do your results tell you?

You can amplify the pulse in your wrist so that the pulse wave that travels along the radial artery can be seen. Place your forearm on a table, palm side up. Put a small lump of clay on the skin that lies directly over the point where you feel your strongest pulse. Stick a straw in the clay as shown in Figure 18b. Watch the top of the straw. You will see it move with each beat of your heart.

You can find a pulse on any artery that is close to the surface of the body. For example, you can feel the pulsing of the carotid arteries in your neck on either side of your Adam's apple (larynx). With a stethoscope, you can listen to the blood flowing through your carotid arteries. Describe the sound.

You can also feel (and sometimes see) the pulse of the temporal artery just in front of your ear. In what other places on your body can you find a pulse? If you find a pulse at a point on the left side of your body, can you always find a pulse on the corresponding point on the right side?

Place the fingers of one hand on a friend's wrist pulse. Place the fingers of your other hand on the pulse in front of your friend's ear. Do you expect to feel both pulses at the same time or to feel one pulse before the other? What do you find? How can you explain the results of this experiment?

If you take your friend's pulse at both his neck and his wrist, which pulse do you expect to feel first? Try it. Were you right?

Exploring on Your Own

Using an anatomy book, identify the major arteries and veins of the human body. After studying these vessels, where might you expect to find pulses?

3-3

The Effect of Body Position and Exercise on Heart Rate

Things you will need:

• clock or watch

• 1, 2, or 3 partners

• pen or pencil

• notebook

• graph paper

(To save time you may wish to combine this experiment with the next one or two experiments. With one partner to measure breathing rate, another to measure pulse rate, and a third to take blood pressure, data for all three experiments can be obtained and recorded at the same time.)

Lie on your back on a couch or floor and rest quietly for five minutes. Then have someone take your pulse to determine how many times your heart beats in one minute. Counting the number of heartbeats over a 30-second period and multiplying by two will give your heart rate in beats per minute. Record that number—your heart rate while lying on your back—in a notebook.

Next, sit up for five minutes. Again, your partner will determine and record your pulse. What is your normal heart rate while sitting?

Now stand up for five minutes. Again, your partner will determine and record your heart rate while standing. How rapidly does your heart beat while you are standing?

Run in place for five minutes. As soon as you stop running, have your partner take your pulse. After recording your heart rate immediately after exercise, have your partner take your pulse and record your heart rate at one-minute intervals until it returns to the rate you had before exercising.

Plot a graph of your heart rate in beats per minute versus time in minutes for the period following your exercise. What can you conclude from the graph?

3-4
The Effect of Body Position and Exercise on Breathing Rate

Things you will need:

- clock or watch
- 1, 2, or 3 partners
- pen or pencil
- notebook

Lie on your back on a couch or floor and rest quietly for five minutes. After that time, have your partner watch your chest to determine how many times you breathe in one minute. (Your chest moves up slightly each time you inhale.) In a notebook, record that data, which is your breathing rate while lying on your back.

Next, sit up and remain seated for five minutes. Again, have your partner determine your breathing rate after that time. Record the data. What is your normal breathing rate while sitting?

Then stand up and remain standing for five minutes. Again, your partner will determine your breathing rate after that time. Record the data. What is your breathing rate when standing?

Next, run in place for five minutes. As soon as you stop running, have your partner determine the number of breaths you take in 30 seconds. How can you record that measurement as breaths per minute?

Have your partner determine your breathing rate at one-minute intervals until your breathing rate returns to the rate you had before exercising. Record all the data.

Plot a graph of breathing rate in breaths per minute versus time in minutes for the period following your exercise. What can you conclude from the graph?

3-5*
The Effect of Body Position and Exercise on Blood Pressure

Pressure is defined as force divided by area. For example, the pressure you exert on the floor is your weight divided by the area of your shoes that touches the floor. Blood pressure is the pressure that blood exerts against the walls of blood vessels. The blood pressure in arteries is greatest when the heart is contracting and forcing more blood into these vessels.

Things you will need:

- battery-powered automatic blood-pressure device or sphygmomanometer
- 1, 2, or 3 partners
- pen or pencil
- notebook
- clock or watch
- graph paper

When someone determines your blood pressure, they measure both systolic and diastolic pressure. Systolic pressure occurs as the heart contracts, forcing blood into the arteries. Diastolic pressure occurs just before the heart contracts, when the pressure in the arteries is at its minimum value. The systolic pressure is recorded first, followed by the diastolic pressure.

A normal record of blood pressure might read 120/70. The pressures are measured in millimeters (mm) of mercury. The pressure of the earth's atmosphere at sea level, which we measure with a barometer, is normally 760 mm of mercury. This means that the air can support a column of mercury 760 mm high, which is the same pressure as 10.1 newtons per square centimeter or 14.7 pounds per square inch. Of course, blood, like the rest of your body, is subject to air pressure. Consequently, blood pressure is the pressure by which the blood exceeds the pressure of the air.

Knowing the systolic and diastolic blood pressure, you can easily calculate what is known as pulse pressure. It is the difference between systolic and diastolic blood pressure. In the example given above, the pulse pressure would be

120 – 70 = 50 mm of mercury.

The easiest way to measure blood pressure is with a battery-operated monitor that fits over the subject's index finger or wrist. It provides a digital display of both systolic and diastolic pressure. A different kind of battery-powered blood-pressure monitor inflates at the press of a button and gives a digital display of blood pressure and pulse rate. Your family may have such an instrument, or you may be able to borrow one.

The more traditional device for measuring blood pressure is the sphygmomanometer found in doctors' offices. It is more difficult to operate than the automatic devices. It consists of a cuff that is placed around the subject's upper arm and then inflated. When the pressure in the cuff exceeds the pressure of the blood flowing through the brachial artery in the upper arm, the artery collapses and blood flow stops. By slowly reducing the pressure in the cuff, a point is reached at which systolic pressure allows a spurt of blood to pass through the artery. The short spurt of blood produces a sound. The sound can be heard by placing a stethoscope over the artery below the cuff on the inside of the elbow. When the first sound is heard, the pressure is read on a gauge, or manometer, attached to the cuff.

As the pressure in the cuff is reduced further, the sound becomes more muffled and eventually disappears. The sound disappears when the cuff no longer restricts any blood flow. Consequently, it indicates the subject's diastolic or minimum blood pressure.

If possible, use one of the automatic blood-pressure devices. If you have to use a sphygmomanometer, **ask an adult** familiar with taking blood pressure to help you. **Be sure that the cuff does not restrict a subject's blood flow for more than a few seconds.**

63

Ask a partner to help you with this experiment. Lie on your back on a couch or floor and rest quietly for five minutes. After that time, your partner will determine your blood pressure. Record the pressure in a notebook. What was your blood pressure while lying down? What was your pulse pressure?

Next, sit up for five minutes. Again, your partner can determine your blood pressure. Record that data. What were your blood pressure and pulse pressure while sitting?

Now stand up for five minutes. After that time, your partner will again determine your blood pressure and pulse pressure. Record the data. What were your blood pressure and pulse pressure after standing?

Finally, exercise by running in place for five minutes. As soon as you stop running, sit down and have your partner determine your blood pressure. Record the blood pressure. Your partner should continue to measure your blood pressure at one-minute intervals until it returns to the pressure you had before exercising. Record all the data.

Plot a graph of your blood pressure versus time for the period following your exercise. Plot a similar graph of your pulse pressure versus time for the period following your exercise. What can you conclude from the graphs?

Exploring on Your Own

Measure the breathing and heart rates and blood pressures of a number of different people after they have been lying, sitting, standing, and exercising for five minutes. Does a subject's age or sex seem to affect the results? Do you notice differences in your data for people who are in good physical shape, such as athletes, and for people who are not "in shape"? If you do, what are those differences and how can you account for them?

3-6
Returning to the Heart

After blood pumped from the heart passes through the arteries and capillaries, it begins its journey back to the heart. The vessels that carry blood to the

Things you will need:

• back of your hand or forearm where veins can be seen clearly

heart are called veins. The pressure in these vessels is much less than it is in the arteries. In fact, without the contraction of skeletal muscles that squeeze the veins, blood tends to collect in the veins of the lower body. To prevent blood from draining down into the legs instead of moving toward the heart, veins contain one-way valves. These valves allow blood to move only one way—toward the heart.

You can find these valves quite easily because many veins lie near the surface of the body. You can see them through your skin. They have a bluish tint. In fact, they sometimes bulge along the skin on the back of your hand or on your forearm. If you have difficulty seeing a vein, let your arm hang down for a few moments so that blood collects in these veins.

Once you can see your veins clearly, put your index finger on one of the veins in your forearm or the back of your hand. Then sweep the blood in the vein toward the heart by moving your thumb along the vein. Gradually increase the distance you move your thumb. When you reach a valve, the vein below the valve will collapse and become difficult to see when you lift your thumb. You will be able to see the blood-filled vein above the valve but not below it. When you release your finger, blood will again flow through the vein. Can you locate the next valve along the vein?

Let your hand hang by your side for a few seconds. When you can clearly see the veins on the back of one hand, slowly raise that hand. What happens when your hand is slightly above your heart? Can you explain why?

Hold one hand over your head for 20 seconds. Let the other one hang at your side. Then look at the back of both hands. One hand will have more color than the other. Which one is it? Why does it have more color than the other?

You can use this difference in skin color to make people think you are psychic. Turn so that your back is toward a person who will serve as the subject of the "psychic" experiment. Tell that subject to place a coin in one hand. Then tell him or her to hold that fist against his or her forehead so that he or she can send waves from his or her brain to yours.

Finally, tell the subject to hold both fists in front of his or her body and you will identify the hand that holds the coin.

You will have to repeat this several times to convince the audience of your psychic powers. You may even have to change subjects.

3-7*
How You Breathe

Things you will need:

- cloth measuring tape
- a friend
- pen or pencil
- notebook

Place a cloth measuring tape around a friend's chest at armpit level. What happens to the circumference of his chest when he takes a deep breath? What happens to the circumference of his chest when he expires as much air as possible?

Now place the tape measure around his abdomen at belly button (navel) level. What happens to the circumference of his abdomen when he takes a deep breath? What happens to it after he expires as much air as possible?

Design a means of measuring the front-to-back thickness of your friend's chest and abdomen following a deep inhalation and a forceful expiration.

As you have seen, your abdomen and chest both grow in circumference when you inhale. Your diaphragm (see Figure 19), which separates your chest and abdominal cavities, contracts, pushing your stomach and other organs in your abdomen downward. At the same time, the intercostal muscles in your chest lift your ribs upward and outward. The result of these movements increases the size of your chest and lungs. The increased volume reduces the air pressure in your lungs, which causes the air pressure outside your body to be greater than the pressure inside. As a result, air is forced into your lungs. This inhaled air travels along the trachea and bronchi (bronchial tubes), which branch into smaller and smaller tubes that finally end in tiny air sacs called alveoli. The alveoli are surrounded by capillaries. It is through these capillaries that oxygen enters the blood. It is there, too, that carbon dioxide passes from blood to air in the alveoli.

When you exhale, just the opposite happens. The rib cage falls, the diaphragm rises, and the air pressure in your lungs increases

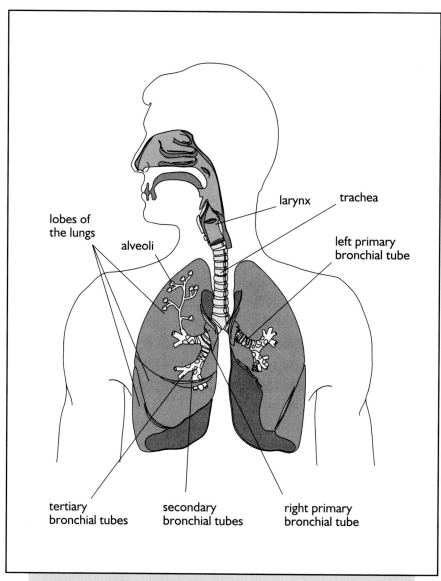

lobes of
the lungs

alveoli

larynx   trachea

left primary
bronchial tube

tertiary
bronchial tubes

secondary
bronchial tubes

right primary
bronchial tube

Figure 19. Air passes from your mouth or nose to your trachea, bronchial tubes, and eventually to the alveoli, where gases (oxygen and carbon dioxide) are exchanged between blood and air.

until it exceeds the air pressure outside. Then air is forced out of your lungs: you exhale.

Often when you have a cold, your nose is filled with mucus. Fortunately, you are still able to breathe. Hold your nose. Can you still breathe? How does the air reach your lungs? Now close your mouth. How does the air reach your lungs? What must be true about your mouth and nose?

Exploring on Your Own

What causes hiccups? How are they related to breathing? There are lots of "cures" for hiccups. Do any of them work?

3-8*
A Model of Your Lungs

You can make a model to show how we breathe. **Ask an adult** to help you cut off the bottom of a clear plastic bottle. **Ask the same adult** to insert a glass or plastic tube through a one-hole rubber stopper, cork, or lump of modeling clay. Use a rubber band to fasten the neck of a balloon to the lower end of the tube. The balloon represents a lung. Insert the stopper, cork, or clay into the mouth of the bottle

Things you will need:

- an adult
- sharp knife or shears
- clear plastic soda bottle
- glass or plastic tube
- one-hole rubber stopper or cork or lump of modeling clay
- rubber bands
- balloon
- rubber dam or a large balloon
- scissors

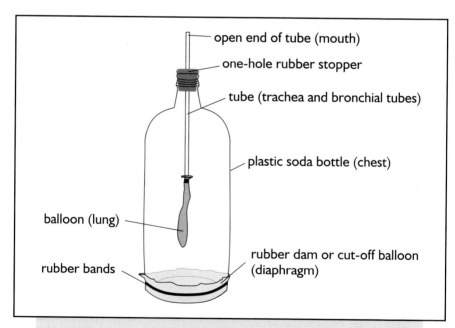

open end of tube (mouth)

one-hole rubber stopper

tube (trachea and bronchial tubes)

plastic soda bottle (chest)

balloon (lung)

rubber bands

rubber dam or cut-off balloon (diaphragm)

Figure 20. You can make a model that shows how we breathe. The words in parentheses show what various pieces of the model represent.

as shown in Figure 20. The tube represents the trachea that connects your lungs with your mouth.

To represent the diaphragm, fasten a rubber dam or the lower two thirds of a large balloon to the bottom of the bottle using long, strong rubber bands.

What happens to the balloon (lung) inside the bottle (chest cavity) when you pull down on the diaphragm? Why does it happen? What happens when you release the diaphragm? Why does it happen?

Exploring on Your Own

Build a better model that includes two lungs and both a diaphragm and the ribs that move up and out during inspiration.

Find out what happens to the lungs when the chest cavity is opened during open-heart surgery.

3-9*
How Much Air Do You Breathe?

Using a stethoscope, listen as air moves through a friend's larynx and trachea. Can you hear air move if you place the stethoscope on the back, front, and sides of your friend's chest as he breathes quietly? Listen again at the same places as your friend breathes deeply. Can you hear air rushing along the bronchial tubes that lead to the alveoli in the lungs (see Figure 19)?

Have your friend exercise vigorously for five minutes. Then listen to your friend's chest area again through the stethoscope. How are the sounds you hear different from the ones you heard before?

Doctors measure the volume of air that you breathe with a device known as a spirometer. Reasonably accurate measurements can be made with a plastic bag and a container of water.

Things you will need:

- stethoscope
- a friend
- 2 large, rigid, transparent or semitransparent plastic containers, one with a volume of about 3–4 L or 1 gal, another about twice as large
- tape
- marking pen
- large graduated cylinder or measuring cup
- 1-L or 1-qt plastic bag
- twistie
- clock or watch
- calculator (optional)
- pen or pencil
- notebook
- 2-L or 2-qt plastic bag
- 5–8-L or 2-gal plastic bag
- several people of different ages, genders, heights, weights, and chest sizes

The volume of air you normally inhale and exhale is called your tidal air. The additional air that you can inhale after taking in a normal breath is called your complemental air. It is the extra air you inhale when you take a deep breath. The volume of air you can exhale after a normal expiration of tidal air is called your supplemental air. Even after forcing out your supplemental air, about 1.2 liters (1.3 quarts) of air remains. This is your residual air.

To measure your tidal air, calibrate a large, rigid, transparent or semitransparent plastic container. Place a narrow strip of tape vertically along the side of the container. Then pour known volumes of water into the container and mark the water levels of the different volumes with a marking pen.

Pour some water into the container until the water level is on one of the lines you marked. Hold your nose so that all the air you breathe goes through your mouth. When you have adjusted to mouth breathing, place the opening of a 1-L or 1-qt plastic bag (from which all the air has been removed) firmly around your mouth just before you exhale. Collect the exhaled air in the bag. (Do not blow, just exhale in a normal way.) Twist the neck of the bag to seal off the exhaled air, and secure it with a twistie. **Caution: Never pull a plastic bag over your head.**

Hold the bag of air in your hand and push it under the water in the calibrated container, as shown in Figure 21a. Mark the water level in the container before and after submerging the bag. Also mark your wrist at the water level. Finally, squeeze all the air out of the bag, hold it in your fist, and put your fist back into the water up to the mark on your wrist (Figure 21b). What is the volume of your hand and the empty bag? How can you find the volume of your tidal air?

Determine your breathing rate by counting the number of times you breathe in one minute. Repeat this several times and take an average. From all your data, what volume of air do you breathe in one day?

After exhaling your normal tidal air, place a 2-L or 2-qt plastic bag firmly around your mouth and exhale as much additional air as possible into the bag. What is the volume of your supplemental air?

Vital Capacity

For this experiment, you will need a calibrated container that is about twice as large as the one you have been using. Once you have

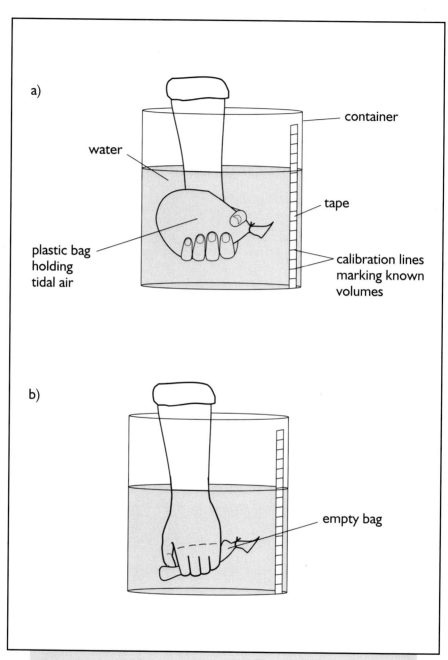

a)

container

water

tape

plastic bag
holding
tidal air

calibration lines
marking known
volumes

b)

empty bag

Figure 21. This experiment will allow you to measure the volume of the air you breathe.

calibrated the container, inhale the deepest breath you can. Then exhale as much air as you can into a 5–8-L or 2-gal plastic bag and seal the bag. How can you find the volume of the air you exhaled?

This large volume of air you exhaled is called your vital capacity. Show that it is the sum of your complemental, tidal, and supplemental airs. What is your vital capacity?

From all your measurements, what is the maximum volume of air that your lungs can hold? (Don't forget the 1.2 liters of residual air.)

Compare the vital capacities of a number of people. Are these volumes related to age? To gender? To height or weight? To chest size?

How about breathing rate? Is it related to age or gender? (Be sure to measure a baby's breathing rate.) Is it related to activity? How do sleep and exercise affect breathing rate?

Exploring on Your Own

How did scientists determine the volume of residual air?

3-10*
Air, Lung Air, and Carbon Dioxide

Because matches are involved in this experiment, it should be done only under adult supervision.

You may have heard that you inhale oxygen and exhale carbon dioxide. However, oxygen makes up only 21 percent of the air. Consequently, you don't inhale *pure* oxygen. Do you exhale pure carbon dioxide?

One way to test the carbon dioxide content of exhaled air is to compare the time that a candle will burn in a volume of air and in the same volume of air from your lungs. To carry out this experiment, use a small piece of clay to support a birthday candle (Figure 22a). **Under adult supervision,** light the candle. After it has been burning for about 15 seconds, invert an empty one-quart jar and place it over the candle, as shown in Figure 22b. Use a clock or a watch that can measure seconds to find out how long the candle will burn in the air-filled jar. Record the time the candle burned after being covered. What finally causes it to go out?

To see how long the candle will burn in lung air, **under adult supervision**, relight the candle, or light a new one of the same size.

Things you will need:

- clay
- birthday candles
- an adult
- matches
- 1-L or 1-qt jar
- clock or watch that can measure seconds
- water
- cardboard square
- pan
- balloon
- limewater, which is a solution of calcium hydroxide— $Ca(OH)_2$ (borrow from school or buy from science supply house or possibly a pharmacy)
- 2 small flasks, about 200 mL each
- 2 two-hole rubber stoppers to fit mouth of flasks
- glass tubing with right-angle bends
- paper bag

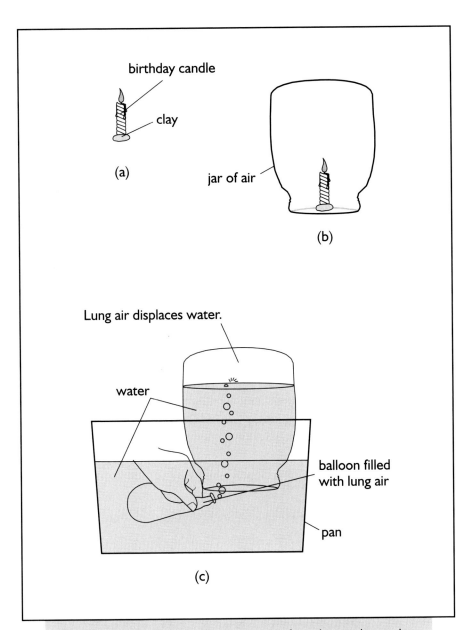

Figure 22. a) A birthday candle will burn in air for as long as the wax lasts. b) How long will the candle burn in a liter- or quart-jar of air? c) Fill the jar with lung air you collect in a balloon. How long will the candle burn in the same volume of lung air?

Then fill the jar with water, cover its mouth with a square piece of cardboard, and invert it in a pan of water. Next, take a breath and immediately use the lung air in that breath to fill a balloon. Seal the neck of the balloon with your fingers. Then place the balloon's mouth under the mouth of the water-filled jar, and let the lung air escape into the jar (Figure 22c). The lung air will replace the water in the jar. Continue to put lung air in the jar until all the water is replaced. Once the jar is filled with air, remove it from the water and place it over the burning candle. For how long will the candle burn in lung air? Record the result.

Repeat the experiment, but this time hold the air in your lungs for about 20 seconds before you use it to fill the balloon. How long will the candle burn in lung air that has been in your lungs for about 20 seconds? Is the candle's burn time different from when you filled the balloon with lung air immediately after it had been inhaled? Can you explain this result?

Carbon Dioxide in Inhaled and Exhaled Air

Carbon dioxide reacts with limewater [a solution of calcium hydroxide—$Ca(OH)_2$] to form a milky white precipitate of chalk (calcium carbonate—$CaCO_3$). You can use limewater to compare the carbon dioxide concentration in inhaled and exhaled air.

First, place about 100 mL of limewater in each of two small flasks that are sealed with two-hole rubber stoppers (Figure 23a). Note and record the time. Then, place your mouth around the shorter tube of one flask, as shown in Figure 23b, and inhale air through your mouth.

The inspired air will have to pass through the limewater before reaching your mouth. Expire the same air through the tube that has its end below the limewater in the second flask, as shown in Figure 23c. Continue to inhale and exhale air in this way. In which flask does the limewater turn milky first? How long did it take?

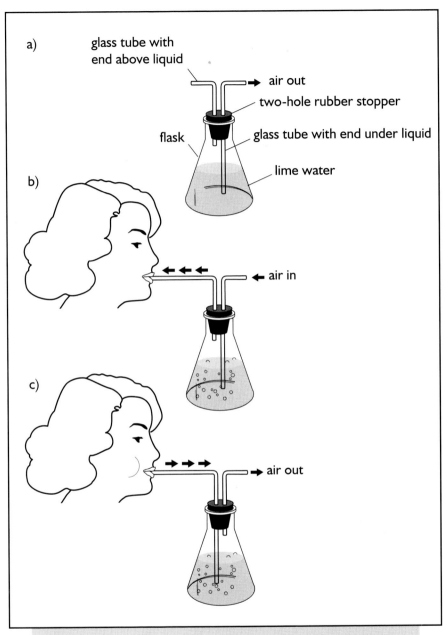

a) glass tube with end above liquid

air out

two-hole rubber stopper

flask

glass tube with end under liquid

lime water

b)

air in

c)

air out

Figure 23. a) Limewater is placed in a flask. b) Inhale air through your mouth from the shorter tube so that the air has to pass through the longer tube and the limewater. c) In the same way, exhale air from your mouth through the longer tube so that air from your lungs has to pass through the limewater into a second identical flask.

Continue to inhale and exhale air through the limewater until the limewater in the other flask turns milky. How long does that take?

The concentration of carbon dioxide in the air you inhale is about 0.04 percent. Based on your data, estimate the concentration of carbon dioxide in the air you exhale.

Effect of Rebreathing Air

What will happen to your breathing rate and depth of breathing if you repeatedly breathe the same air? To find out, **under adult supervision**, place the opening of a paper bag tightly around your nose and mouth so that no fresh air can reach your lungs. Breathe and rebreathe the air in the bag for a minute or two. What happens to your breathing rate? What happens to your depth of breathing (the volume of air you take into your lungs with each breath)? Can you explain the changes that occur?

Exploring on Your Own

Ordinary air is about 21 percent oxygen and 0.04 percent carbon dioxide. The concentration of nitrogen in both inhaled and exhaled air is 78 percent. Design and carry out an experiment to determine the percentage of oxygen and carbon dioxide in exhaled tidal air.

4

The Digestive and Excretory Systems

Food that you ingest (eat) is processed by your digestive system. This system begins in your mouth, where you chew and partially digest food (see Figure 24). Chewing increases the surface area of the food and, therefore, puts more of the food in contact with digestive juices in the mouth, stomach, and intestine. After being swallowed, food passes along your esophagus to your stomach, and from there to your small intestine, where most of the food is digested and absorbed. Digestion involves the chemical breakdown of the large molecules found in food (carbohydrates, fats, and proteins) into smaller molecules. This is accomplished by enzymes and liquids secreted by your salivary glands, liver, stomach, pancreas, and small intestine.

After digestion, the small molecules are monosaccharide sugars from carbohydrates, amino acids from proteins, and fatty acids and glycerol from fats. These molecules can pass through your intestinal membranes, enter your blood, and be carried to the cells of your body. Food that cannot be digested and absorbed into the

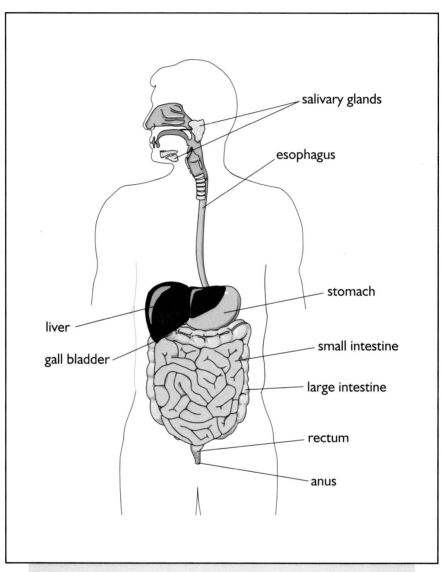

Figure 24. The major organs in your digestive system.

blood passes into the large intestine and becomes the waste that is excreted as feces.

Teeth

Your teeth break food into small particles for swallowing and easier digestion. Teeth are not bones. In fact, the outer layer of the visible part of your teeth—the enamel—comes from the same embryonic tissue as your skin. Like bones, your teeth are very hard—particularly the enamel, which is the hardest substance in the human body. As a result, fossil teeth, some of them more than a million years old, are the most commonly found evidence of early human-like species. Information about the types of teeth and the age at which each type typically appears is provided in Table 1.

Table 1: Number of human teeth and the age at which each type typically appears.

BABY TEETH	Molars	Canines	Incisors
Upper jaw	4	2	4
Lower jaw	4	2	4

6–9 months: lower central incisors   16–20 months: canines
8–10 months: upper incisors   20–24 months: second molars
15–21 months: lower outer incisors
     and first molars

PERMANENT TEETH	Molars	Premolars	Canines	Incisors
Upper jaw	6 (2–3 roots)	4 (1 or 2 roots)	2 (1 root)	4 (1 root)
Lower jaw	6 (2–3 roots)	4 (1 or 2 roots)	2 (1 root)	4 (1 root)

6–7 years: first molars, central incisors   10–12 years: second premolars
7–8 years: outer incisors   11–13 years: second molars
9–10 years: first premolars   17–25 years: third molars
9–12 years: canines   (wisdom teeth)

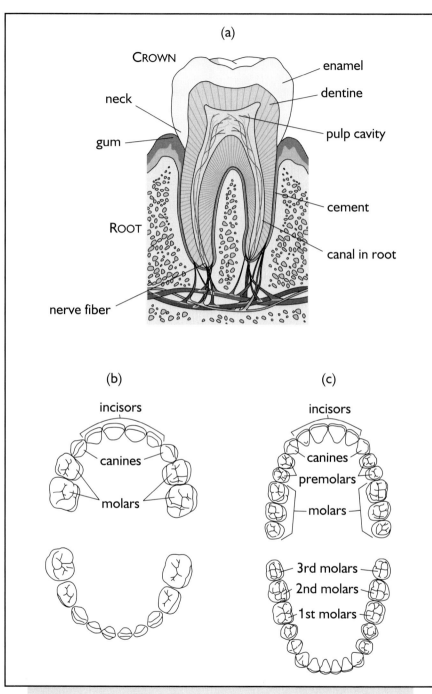

Figure 25. a) The inside of a molar tooth. Blood vessels and nerve cells are found in the pulp cavity. b) The 20 teeth of a child. c) The 32 permanent adult teeth.

Your teeth are embedded in your mandible and maxilla bones. Each tooth (see Figure 25a) has a visible enamel-covered crown, a neck that lies under the crown, and a root or roots that are embedded in the jawbones. The bulk of a tooth is dentine, or ivory. Dentine in the roots is covered by bonelike cement. At the center of each tooth is a pulp cavity that extends into each root through a canal. The canal opens at the base of each root, and it is through this opening that blood vessels and nerve fibers enter the pulp cavity.

Humans are born toothless, but they develop two sets of teeth during early life. The first set, known as deciduous, or baby, teeth, consists of 20 teeth (Figure 25b): 10 in the mandible and 10 in the maxilla. There are 32 teeth in the second or permanent set of teeth (Figure 25c), 16 in each jawbone.

4-1*
A Look at Teeth and Teeth in Action

Examine the teeth of a young child, such as a younger sibling, between the ages of two and six. Ask the child's parent for permission to do this. Usually, children are happy to let you look at their teeth, but if they are unwilling, do not force them.

Things you will need:

- child between the ages of two and six
- an adult
- small piece of cooked steak
- apple

Can you identify all 20 of the child's teeth? Can you also see other structures in the mouth such as tongue, tonsils, and uvula? (See Figure 26.)

Next, ask an adult, such as a parent, if you can look into his or her mouth. Can you identify all 32 adult teeth? Often, one or more third molars will be missing. People frequently have their third molars, or wisdom teeth, removed. How do incisors, canines,

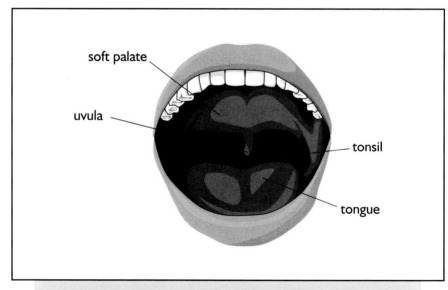

Figure 26. The soft palate, uvula, and tonsils can be seen in a person's mouth.

premolars, and molars differ in size and shape? Do any of the teeth have fillings? Have any of them been capped?

Can you also see other structures in the mouth such as tongue, tonsils, and uvula?

What role do incisors, canines, premolars, and molars play in preparing food for swallowing? To find out, you will need an apple and a piece of cooked steak that has not been cut into bite-sized pieces. Begin with the steak. Which teeth do you use to tear the meat apart? Which teeth do you use to grind the meat into tiny pieces you can swallow?

Next, bite a piece from the apple. Which teeth do you use to bite into the apple and cut away a piece of it? Which teeth do you use to grind up the apple?

You learned earlier that the jaw is a hinge joint. Notice that your mandible can move sideways as well as up and down. How does the ability of your jaw to move sideways help you to prepare food for swallowing?

Exploring on Your Own

Why are premolar and molar teeth often referred to as bicuspids and tricuspids, respectively?

Does the uvula, which hangs from the rear of the soft palate, have any function?

Compare human teeth with the teeth of other primates and other mammals. Explain how the differences you find in the structure and arrangement of their teeth are related to the food the animals eat.

What happens when a person gets a root canal?

4-2
Can You Swallow While Upside Down?

There are involuntary muscles surrounding your stomach and intestine. The contraction of these muscles, known as peristalsis, pushes food, both digestible and indigestible, along your gastrointestinal tract.

Things you will need:
- glass of water
- drinking straw
- chair

Normally when you swallow food or liquids, you are sitting at a table. It seems reasonable to assume that gravity would cause the food you swallow to move down your esophagus to your stomach.

On the other hand, astronauts aboard the space shuttle are able to swallow food under conditions of weightlessness. Perhaps there are smooth muscles along the esophagus that move food by peristalsis. This experiment will help you decide whether or not peristalsis exists in the esophagus.

Place a glass of water with a drinking straw on the floor next to a chair. Place your stomach on the seat of the chair and lean over so that you can reach the straw with your mouth. Be certain that your mouth is well below your stomach. Can you drink the water while your stomach and esophagus are above your mouth? What do you conclude about peristalsis in the esophagus?

4-3
Listening to a Swallow

Having seen that you can swallow liquid while upside down, you might wonder how long it takes a peristaltic wave to travel along the length of your esophagus. To find out, place the chest piece of a stethoscope on a friend's abdomen about an inch below the xiphoid process (see

Things you will need:

- stethoscope
- a friend
- glass of water
- stopwatch or watch with a second hand or mode
- ruler

p. 20). Have the friend swallow a sip of water. At the moment she swallows the water, have her start a stopwatch or note the exact time on a watch with a second hand or mode.

You will hear the water splash against the closed cardiac sphincter that separates the esophagus from the stomach. A short time later, when the peristaltic wave reaches the sphincter, you will hear the water pass through the opening into the stomach. When you hear that second sound, say, "Stop!" When your partner hears that word, she will stop the watch or note the exact time on a watch with a second hand or mode.

How long did it take for the peristaltic wave to pass along the length of the esophagus? How can you use that time and another measurement to estimate the speed at which the peristaltic wave traveled along the esophagus?

4-4*
Digesting Starch

Starch is a carbohydrate, which is one of the three basic foods; the other two are fats and proteins. If you add iodine to starch, a dark blue compound is formed. The color serves as a positive test for starch. You can see this color change by adding a drop of tincture of iodine to starch or to foods that contain starch.

In separate medicine cups or vials, place small amounts of cornstarch, raw potato, soda cracker, and white bread. Add a drop of tincture of iodine to each solid. What color change do you see?

The digestion of starch begins in the mouth, where saliva is secreted by salivary glands found in your cheeks. Starch is acted on by amylase, an enzyme found in saliva.

Things you will need:
- medicine cups or vials
- cornstarch
- raw potato
- soda crackers
- white bread
- tincture of iodine
- eyedropper
- lemon juice
- measuring cup or graduated cylinder
- an adult
- small cooking pan
- stove
- sugarless chewing gum
- small test tube or vial
- water
- tape
- thermometer
- plastic wrap
- clock or watch

Salivation: Another Reflex

Collect saliva in your mouth for a period of five minutes. Then spit the saliva into a medicine cup. How much saliva accumulated in your mouth during the five-minute period?

Now use a clean eyedropper to place a few drops of lemon juice on your tongue. Again, measure the volume of saliva that collects during the next five minutes. How do the two volumes you collected compare? What evidence do you have of a reflex response to the presence of lemon juice?

Amylase in Action

To see how the enzyme amylase in saliva affects starch, first prepare a starch solution. Mix one gram (about one teaspoonful) of cornstarch with 100 mL of water. Pour the mixture into a pan and, **under adult supervision**, bring the mixture to a boil on a stove.

While the liquid is heating, chew some sugarless gum to help provide a supply of saliva, which you can spit into a medicine cup. You will use this saliva later in this experiment.

Once the starch-water mixture is boiling, remove it from the stove and let it cool. Use an eyedropper to withdraw about 2 mL of the cooled liquid and place it in a small test tube or vial. Place another 2 mL in an identical test tube. Then add about the same amount of saliva and a drop of tincture of iodine to the liquid in the first test tube. Add 2 mL of water and a drop of tincture of iodine to the second test tube. What color changes do you observe? What causes the color changes?

Use tape to mark the test tube containing the saliva. Then place both tubes in a water bath at body temperature (37°C, or 98.6°F). What is the purpose of the tube with water, starch, and iodine?

Watch the two tubes over the next hour or two. What changes in color do you observe? What can you conclude about the effect of saliva on starch?

Another way to see the action of amylase is to look at its effect on the starch in food. To see this effect, chew a soda cracker for five minutes so that it becomes thoroughly mixed with your saliva. Spit the chewed cracker and saliva into a medicine cup.

With an eyedropper, remove a small amount of the chewed cracker and place it in another medicine cup. Then add a drop of tincture of iodine. What can you conclude? Has all the starch been digested?

Cover the cup that contains the chewed cracker and saliva with a loose piece of plastic wrap. After several hours test another sample of the chewed cracker and saliva with iodine. Continue to test for starch at intervals of about six hours for several days.

Is the starch eventually digested? If it is, how long did it take?

Although the digestion of starch begins in the mouth, it is completed in the intestine, where amylase secreted by the pancreas changes starch to disaccharide sugars. The disaccharides, in turn, are broken into monosaccharide sugars by enzymes secreted from the glands in the wall of the small intestine. What evidence do you have from your experiments that would suggest the digestion of starch is not completed in the mouth?

Exploring on Your Own

What are the various enzymes and liquids involved in digesting the food you eat? What are the source and role of each one?

Excretion

Not all body waste is excreted as feces. As you have already seen, carbon dioxide leaves the blood through the lungs. Water, some of which is a respiratory waste, is excreted as vapor from the lungs. Some is mixed with solids in the feces we defecate. But much of the water is used to dissolve the wastes excreted from our kidneys.

Your kidneys—a pair of reddish brown organs that lie against the back of your abdomen—filter your blood. The filtering process removes waste materials and retains vital elements and compounds essential to your health. Urine is the liquid waste produced by the kidneys. It flows from the kidneys along the ureters to the bladder, where it is stored (see Figure 27). As urine accumulates, the bladder walls stretch, stimulating nerves leading to your brain that indicate the need to urinate. When you urinate, the bladder contracts, forcing urine out of your body through the urethra.

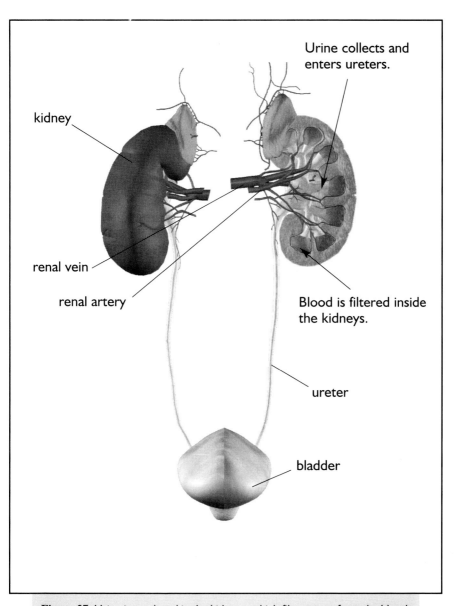

Urine collects and
enters ureters.

kidney

renal vein

renal artery

Blood is filtered inside
the kidneys.

ureter

bladder

Figure 27. Urine is produced in the kidneys, which filter waste from the blood. The urine flows through ureters to the bladder, where it collects. The bladder is emptied periodically.

4-5*
How Much Urine Do You Excrete?

The urine you excrete is 95 percent water. The rest is minerals and nitrogen-rich substances such as urea, uric acid, and ammonia produced by the metabolism of proteins. Although bacteria can contaminate urine, the liquid is normally sterile as it passes from the bladder.

You can determine the volume of urine you excrete each day. Choose a week when you plan to be at home most of the time. Simply collect the liquid in a graduated container such as a large measuring cup or a cylindrical container that you have calibrated. After you record the volume and time in a notebook, empty the urine into a toilet and flush. Then wash your hands.

Things you will need:

• graduated container such as a large measuring cup or a cylinder that you have calibrated

• pen or pencil

• notebook

• toilet

• a friend

• device to measure specific gravity (optional; available from science supply houses or possibly from your school)

• clock or watch

• water

• clear container

• pH paper (range 5–9)

• various chemical test strips (stix) to test for glucose, protein, ketones, white blood cells, bilirubin, and other factors

Do this each day for a week. What is the average volume of urine you excrete daily? Do you find a pattern? For example, do you excrete more urine in the morning than in the afternoon and/or evening?

Do your kidneys respond rapidly or slowly to changes in fluid intake? You can find out by serving as your own subject. Ask a friend to serve as a control. Both you and your friend should empty your bladders at the beginning of this experiment. If you have access to equipment that can measure the specific gravity (density) of urine, you and your friend should measure the specific gravity of both urine samples.

Your friend (the control) will not drink during the experiment. After one hour, your friend will again empty his bladder and measure the volume of urine (and specific gravity). As the subject, you will drink water immediately after urinating. The volume you drink should be 12 milliliters (mL) per kilogram (kg) of body weight, or 5.5 mL per pound (lb). For example, if you weigh 100 pounds, you should drink 100 lb x 5.5 mL/lb, or 550 mL.

You are to empty your bladder and measure the volume (and specific gravity) of your urine at 20-minute intervals. How long does it take to excrete a volume of urine equal to the volume of water you drank? How does the volume of urine you excrete in one hour compare to the volume excreted by the control? How does the color of the two samples compare? If you have measured specific gravities as well, how do they compare?

Testing Urine

Normally urine is a clear, light yellow liquid. Examine a sample of your urine in a clear container. Urine excreted in the morning after a long night's rest may have a deeper color than samples collected during the day. Can you explain why?

Urine that is cloudy, reddish, greenish yellow, or golden brown may indicate disorders that should be checked by a doctor.

If possible, obtain pH paper (range 5–9) and various chemical test strips (stix) from a pharmacy, your school science department, or a science supply house (see List of Suppliers on page 115). The pH paper will allow you to test the acidity of your urine. The various test strips will enable you to test for glucose (common in people with diabetes), protein, ketones, white blood cells, bilirubin, and other factors. What do positive results for any of these tests indicate?

Exploring on Your Own

Design an experiment to find out if weather, particularly temperature, affects the amount of urine you excrete.

5

The Nervous and Endocrine Systems

There are two systems that control and coordinate your body. They are the nervous system and the endocrine system. The hypothalamus, located at the base of the brain, links the two systems. The hypothalamus releases chemicals that affect the pituitary gland, which lies beneath the hypothalamus. The pituitary, in turn, controls many other glands by its release of hormones that stimulate other endocrine glands. For that reason, the pituitary has often been called the master gland.

The Nervous System

Your nervous system controls and coordinates actions that take place in your body. The central nervous system, which consists of the brain and spinal cord, is well protected. The brain is enclosed within the skull, and the spinal cord lies inside the vertebrae that make up the backbone. The nerves that emerge from the central nervous system and connect it with the rest of the body constitute the peripheral nervous system.

Nerve cells (neurons), shown in Figure 28a, respond to stimuli both inside and outside the body. A stimulus causes electrical action—an impulse—that travels in one direction along the nerve cell from dendrite to cell body to axon. Neurons are not connected to one another. There is a gap between the axon of one nerve cell and the dendrites of another. The gap is called a synapse. Chemicals produced at the end of a nerve cell's axon carry an impulse across the synapse to the dendrites of another neuron.

There are three types of neurons: sensory, association, and motor. Sensory neurons carry impulses from sense organs, such as your eyes, ears, nose, and the sensory receptors in your skin and internal organs, to your central nervous system. Association neurons connect sensory and motor neurons. Motor neurons transmit nerve impulses to muscles.

Most impulses that travel along motor neurons arise in the brain. For example, you see a ball that is thrown to you by means of sensory impulses that travel from your eyes to the back of your brain. Association neurons carry these impulses to motor neurons that cause the muscles in your arms to move your hands so that they can catch the ball.

The region of the brain that coordinates the impulses that allow you to catch a ball is the cerebrum (Figure 28b). It is the largest part of the human brain. It is the part concerned with memories, thoughts, learning, speech, and voluntary movements. At the rear of the brain and under the cerebrum is the cerebellum. It coordinates nerve impulses to and from the cerebrum and also controls muscle coordination, including those that keep your body balanced. The medulla, which lies at the base of the brain, controls impulses that regulate such involuntary actions as breathing, heartbeat, and contractions of smooth muscles.

Not all motor impulses arise in the brain. Some are reflex actions—automatic responses to stimuli that arise in a sensory organ. The impulse passes along a sensory neuron to an association

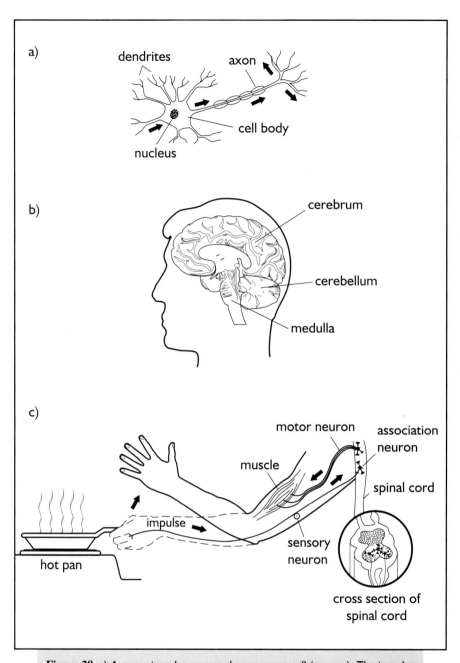

Figure 28. a) A nerve impulse moves along a nerve cell (neuron). The impulse starts in a dendrite. It travels to the cell body and then along an axon to another neuron or muscle. b) The three main parts of the brain are the cerebrum, cerebellum, and medulla, or brain stem. c) Reflexes such as this one can protect you from harm. You touch something hot and immediately pull your hand away. The reflex allows you to react without thinking.

neuron in the spinal cord, and from there to a motor neuron that carries an impulse to a muscle or muscles. You may be aware of a reflex action, but it is automatic. It happens before you have time to think about it. Figure 28c shows a reflex reaction that occurs when you touch something hot.

Normal body functions are maintained or adjusted to meet immediate needs by the autonomic nervous system. Impulses in the autonomic system are below the level of consciousness. Nerve cells that are part of the autonomic system arise in the medulla or spinal cord. There are two divisions to this system, the sympathetic and parasympathetic. The effects of the two divisions generally produce opposite effects on the smooth muscles, heart muscle, and glands that they control. In general, the sympathetic nervous system prepares the body for action in response to stress. The parasympathetic system produces opposite effects and keeps the body in a more relaxed state. Effects of the two systems are summarized in Table 2.

Table 2: Effects of the sympathetic and parasympathetic divisions of the autonomic nervous system.

Sympathetic	Parasympathetic
Dilates pupils of the eyes	Contracts pupils of the eyes
Dilates bronchial tubes	Constricts bronchial tubes
Increases heart rate	Decreases heart rate
Increases strength of heart contractions	Decreases strength of heart contractions
Reduces intestinal movements	Increases intestinal movements
Increases secretions of glands	Decreases secretion of glands

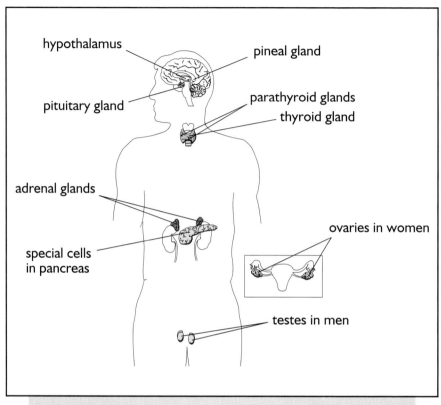

Figure 29. The major organs that make up the body's endocrine system.

The Endocrine System

The endocrine system (Figure 29) is made up of glands that secrete chemical substances known as hormones into the blood. Hormones are chemical "messengers" that cause changes in certain parts of the body. Table 3 provides information about the major endocrine glands.

Table 3. The major endocrine glands, the hormones they produce, and the hormones' effects on the body.

Gland	Hormone(s) Produced	Effect of Hormone
pituitary	GH (growth hormone)	controls growth of body
	gonadotropic hormone	stimulates hormone production in ovaries or testes
	TSH (thyroid-stimulating hormone)	influences thyroid gland
	ACTH (adrenocorticotropic hormone)	influences cortex of adrenal gland
	FSH (follicle-stimulating hormone)	causes eggs to develop in ovary; maintains seminiferous tubules in testes
	LH (luteinizing hormone)	influences ovaries and testes
	ADH (antidiuretic hormone)	controls body's water and salt balance
	oxytocin	stimulates milk production and contractions of the uterus
pineal	melatonin	controls body rhythms such as sleeping
thyroid	thyroxin	controls body's metabolism
	thyrocalcitonin	lowers blood calcium and phosphate
parathyroid	parathyroid hormone	increases blood calcium and phosphate
adrenal: cortex	mineralcorticoids	regulates salt and water balance in body
	cortisone	regulates metabolism of food
medulla	adrenaline (epinephrine)	controls body's response to stress by stimulating carbohydrate metabolism
	noradrenaline (norepinephrine)	controls body's response to stress by increasing heart rate and blood pressure
kidney	erythropoietin	stimulates production of red blood cells
	renin	increases blood flow
pancreas	insulin	reduces blood sugar level
	glucagon	raises blood sugar level
ovary	estrogen	stimulates development of secondary sexual characteristics
	progesterone	prepares uterus for pregnancy
testes	testosterone	causes development of secondary sexual characteristics

5-1*
Testing Reflex Actions

There are many reflex actions that take place in your body. Doctors sometimes test a patient to see if any of the common reflexes are missing. The reason for doing this is that the association neurons responsible for different reflexes are located at different levels in the spinal cord. By determining which reflexes are not working, a doctor can determine the site of nerve damage.

Reflexes that involve the autonomic nervous system are involuntary. You cannot control them by willful muscle action. Reflexes that reach the conscious level of the brain may be controlled by voluntary action, at least to some extent.

With a friend to serve as a subject, you can examine a number of human reflexes. You can also check to see which ones are controlled by the autonomic nervous system.

Things you will need:
- pencil
- large one-hole rubber stopper
- a friend
- table
- clock or watch with second hand or mode
- flashlight
- chair
- sheet of cardboard
- several people of different ages and genders

Patellar Reflex

The reflex with which you are probably most familiar is the knee jerk. It is the one your doctor checks when you have a physical examination. He or she probably uses a rubber hammer to hit your lower leg just below the kneecap. You can make your own rubber hammer by inserting a pencil into a large one-hole rubber stopper.

To test this reflex yourself, have a friend sit on a table with her lower leg relaxed and hanging from the edge of the table. Use your rubber hammer to strike your friend's leg just below the kneecap and just above the top of the tibia. This stretches the patellar tendon and should elicit the reflex. The response is the contraction of

102

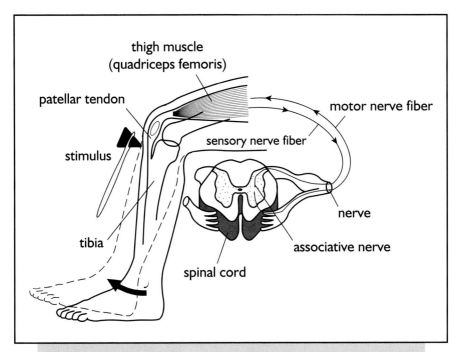

Figure 30. The patellar reflex: stretching the patellar tendon by tapping it is the stimulus for a reflex that causes the thigh muscle to contract, thus raising the lower leg.

the quadriceps muscle, which pulls the lower leg upward (see Figure 30). Can your friend willfully prevent the reflex from happening by tightening her leg muscles?

How does the time for the patellar reflex stimulus to work compare with the voluntary response to a verbal command to kick your leg upward? How can you explain any difference in the time between stimulus and response for these two actions?

Pupillary Reflex

Examine the pupils of your subject's eyes in normal light. Then have her close her eyes for at least one minute. When she opens her eyes, what do you notice about the size of her pupils? What happens to their size once they are in brighter light?

Use a flashlight to shine a light into one eye of your subject. What happens to the size of the pupil in that eye? Does the pupil of

103

the other eye respond in the same way? Can your subject willfully prevent her pupils from responding to changes in light intensity?

Ciliospinal reflex

Watch a subject's pupils as you gently move the hairs on the back of her neck. What happens to the size of the pupils? What happens to the subject's pupils if you pinch the back of her neck?

Blinking reflex

Ask someone to sit quietly in a chair. Without warning, **but with care not to touch the eyes**, wave your hand in front of his face. What happens? Can he willfully control this reflex and not blink?

Have your subject hold a sheet of cardboard about as long as his head perpendicular to the center of his face. The purpose of the cardboard (which should not be known to the subject) is to prevent the air you blow into one eye from reaching the other eye.

With cardboard barrier in place, blow into one eye. Does the eye you blow into blink? Does the other eye blink, too? Can the subject willfully control this reflex and not blink when you blow into one of his eyes?

Exploring on Your Own

Test the reflexes you have examined on a number of different people. Do some respond faster than others? Do the responses vary in any way? Does age or gender seem to affect an individual's reflexes?

Can you find other reflexes that are common to all humans?

With the permission of its parent, test the reflexes of a baby that is just a few days old. What happens when you touch the baby's cheek near its mouth? What happens when you place your index finger across the baby's palm? Do these reflexes have any survival value?

What are the Moro and walking reflexes found in babies? Ask the parent of a baby if he or she has seen these reflexes.

5-2*
Measuring Reaction Time

How quickly can you react to a visual stimulus? This experiment will enable you to find out. You will see something start to move. A nerve impulse from your eye will travel to the occipital region of your brain. From there, another impulse will travel to a center in your brain that will, in turn, send impulses

Things you will need:
- desk or table
- one-foot ruler
- a friend
- pen or pencil
- notebook
- several people of different genders and ages
- tape measure

to the muscles of your forearm. You will react by using the muscles in your forearm to bring your thumb and fingers together.

To do the experiment, rest the heel of your hand on the edge of a desk or table as shown in Figure 31. Your thumb and fingers should be about an inch apart. Your friend is to hold a one-foot ruler, which he will drop. He holds it so that the zero end of the ruler is even with your thumb and index finger.

Watch the bottom of the ruler. When your friend releases the ruler, you will see the end of the ruler begin to fall. As soon as you see it begin to fall, bring your thumb and fingers together. How far did the ruler fall before you caught it? You can tell how far it fell by seeing what inch line on the ruler lies under your thumb or index finger. The faster you react, the shorter the distance the ruler will fall.

Record the distance the ruler fell. Then repeat the experiment four more times. For each trial, record the distance the ruler fell. Then calculate the average distance the ruler fell. Use Table 4 to determine the time it took for you to react.

Suppose you catch the ruler at say, 6 ¾ inches. How can you estimate your reaction time?

Based on the data you collected, what was your reaction time?

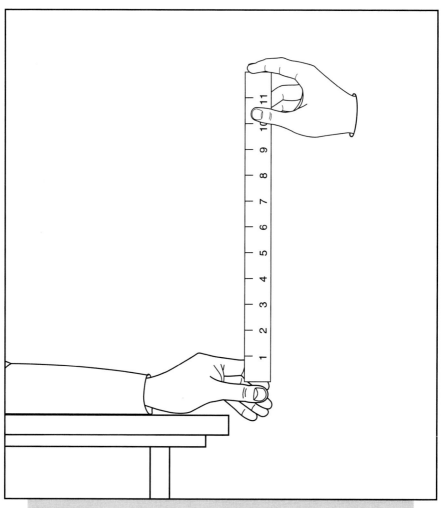

Figure 31. Your reaction time can be determined by measuring the distance a ruler falls before you catch it.

Table 4: Reaction times for various distances a ruler falls before being caught.

Distance ruler fell (inches)	Reaction time (seconds)
1	0.072
2	0.102
3	0.125
4	0.144
5	0.161
6	0.177
7	0.191
8	0.204
9	0.216
10	0.228
11	0.239
12	0.250

Repeat the experiment using your other hand. Does your dominant hand react faster than your other hand?

Repeat the experiment to test your friend's reaction time. How does it compare with yours?

Try the experiment with a number of different people. Choose people of different genders and ages. Measure their reaction times for each of their hands. Does hand dominance affect reaction time? Do girls react faster than boys? Does age affect reaction time?

Your reaction time is related to the time for a visual nerve stimulus to move from your eye to your brain and for another nerve stimulus to travel from your brain to the muscles in your forearm. Using a tape measure and the data you have collected, make an estimate of the speed at which nerve impulses travel along nerve fibers.

Exploring on Your Own

Measure your reaction time at different times of the day, such as just after you get up, just before lunch, late afternoon, and just before going to bed. Does time of day affect your reaction time? If it does, can you explain why?

Explain how the reaction times for different distances of fall in Table 4 were determined.

5-3*
Your Biased Brain

Things you will need:
- several people
- distant object you can see
- a friend
- clock or watch with second hand or mode
- pen or pencil
- notebook

Nerve impulses leading to the muscles that allow you to voluntarily move your body originate in your brain. But your brain is biased. Most people use their right hand to write, throw a ball, eat, and do most tasks that require fine-motor movements. We say these people are right-handed, or that their right hand is their dominant hand. About one in every ten people is left-handed. For some reason, the brains of these people provide better fine-motor impulses to the muscles of the left hand than to the right. (There are a few people who can use either hand equally well. They are said to be ambidextrous.)

In this experiment, you can tell whether a person is right- or left-handed without asking them to write or throw a ball. Ask a number of people to serve as subjects. Table 5 shows the tasks you can ask them to do and the observations you could make.

From the way your subjects perform these tasks, how can you tell whether they are right- or left-handed? If a subject has mixed results, he or she has some ability to use both hands with ease and is ambidextrous.

Most people have a dominant eye. To find out which eye is your dominant eye, keep both eyes open as you align the thumb of your outstretched arm with some distant object. Now close first one eye and then the other. For which eye is your thumb actually aligned with the distant object? Which eye is your dominant eye?

Ask several people to try this same experiment. For what percentage of people is the right eye the dominant one? For how many was the left eye the dominant eye? Do right-handed people tend to be right-eyed and left-handed people left-eyed?

Table 5: Tasks to observe to determine if a person is right- or left-handed.

Task you ask subject to perform	What to observe
Fold your hands together.	Which thumb is on top?
Cross your arms.	Which hand is on top of the opposite arm?
Clasp your hands behind your back.	Which hand is the clasping hand?
Draw a profile of a face.	In which direction is the face turned?

Habits

Some actions are repeated so many times that they become routine. The nerve impulses needed to move the muscles that perform the job become almost automatic. We perform the task with little need to think about what we are doing.

One action that becomes habitual is signing your name. To see how a habitual task compares with a task that requires attention and concentration, try this. Have a friend note and record the time it takes you to sign your name ten times. Then have him measure the time it takes for you to write your name backwards ten times. What can you conclude?

Exploring on Your Own

If asked to read a passage with one eye, do people read better with their dominant eye? Design an experiment to find out.

Do people have a dominant foot as well as a dominant hand? Design an experiment to find out.

Do people have a dominant ear? Design an experiment to find out.

5-4

The Hypothalamus and Body Temperature

The hypothalamus is your body's thermostat. It responds to the temperature of blood by sending impulses to blood vessels in the skin. The impulses direct these vessels to dilate or contract. By dilating, they bring more warm blood close to the body's surface and thereby cool the body by increasing heat loss through the skin. By contracting, they reduce heat losses. How do you think impulses from the hypothalamus might affect the heart as a means of responding to body temperature?

Things you will need:
- a friend
- shower
- thermometer to measure body temperature (digital or mercury)
- thermometer to measure air temperature
- pen or pencil
- notebook
- clock or watch
- lab thermometer
- ice water
- device to measure blood pressure

To see how your hypothalamus controls body temperature, you can take a hot shower and record your body temperature, heart rate, and air temperature at different times during the shower. You can then continue to take data on your temperature and heart rate as you cool off after the shower.

Prepare a data table similar to Table 6. Ask a friend outside the shower to watch the time and record data in the table you have prepared.

Before entering the shower, place a thermometer that can measure air temperature in the bathroom. Place a digital or mercury thermometer under your tongue for two minutes. (If you use a mercury mouth thermometer, have your partner shake down the liquid until the mercury reading is below 35°C, or 95°F.) During the second minute, take your pulse to obtain your heart rate. After two minutes remove and read the thermometer, and have your friend record your temperature, heart rate, and room temperature in the data table.

If you are using a mercury thermometer, have your partner shake down the thermometer liquid again before entering the shower and each time before you take your temperature. To avoid slippery hands, which could cause you to drop the thermometer, **do not use soap while taking this shower.**

Place the thermometer in your mouth and observe your skin color as you enter the hot shower. **Be sure to keep the mouth thermometer away from the hot water!** Keep the shower water as hot as possible without feeling uncomfortable. Your partner will let you know when one minute has passed. At that point begin counting your heart beats by taking your pulse. Your partner will again let you know when two minutes have passed. At that time, remove the thermometer and tell him or her your heart rate and your body temperature. Your partner can record that data as well as room temperature.

Your partner will inform you when 4, 5, 9, and 10 minutes have passed so that body temperature, heart rate, and room temperature can be recorded at 5 and 10 minutes after you enter the shower. Between 5 and 7 minutes, if possible, ask your partner to hand you a lab thermometer so that you can measure the temperature of the water in the shower.

After 10 minutes, turn off the shower and open the bathroom window or door so that the air around you cools. Observe your skin color and record heart rate, body temperature, and room temperature at 2, 4, and 6 minutes after coming out of the shower.

Compare the changes in room temperature with changes in body temperature. Compare body temperatures with the hot water's temperature.

How did your skin color before and immediately after the shower compare? What can you conclude?

To see how the hypothalamus responds to a falling temperature, have a subject sit quietly in a room at a comfortable temperature

Table 6: Data table to see how body temperature and heart rate respond to changes in temperature.

Time (min)	Body temp.	Heart rate (beats/min)	Room temp.	Air temp. in shower	Water temp.
Before shower					
During shower					
2					
5					
10					
After shower					
2					
4					
6					

when it is very cool or cold outside. Record the subject's body temperature, heart rate (pulse), and blood pressure. Also note her skin color and temperature (warm, cool, or cold). Then turn down the thermostat and open windows to make the room as cool as possible. After a few minutes, again record the subject's body temperature, heart rate, blood pressure, and note her skin color and temperature.

Based on the data you have collected, what signals does the hypothalamus send to the heart and blood vessels of the skin when there is sudden drop in the temperature of the environment?

Instead of placing a subject's entire body in a cold environment, have your subject place her hand in ice water for one minute. Record the subject's body temperature, heart rate, and blood pressure before and at one-minute intervals after she removes her hand from the ice water. Also note her skin color and temperature. Does the body respond differently if only a small part of the body rather than the entire body is exposed to a cold temperature?

List of Suppliers

Carolina Biological Supply Co.
2700 York Road
Burlington, NC 27215
(800) 334-5551
http://www.carolina.com

Central Scientific Co. (CENCO)
3300 Cenco Parkway
Franklin Park, IL 60131
(800) 262-362
http://www.cenconet.com

**Connecticut Valley Biological
Supply Co., Inc.**
82 Valley Road, Box 326
Southampton, MA 01073
(800) 628-7748
Delta Education
P.O. Box 915
Hudson, NH 03051-0915
(800) 258-1302

Edmund Scientific Co.
101 East Gloucester Pike
Barrington, NJ 08007
(609) 547-3488

Educational Innovations, Inc.
151 River Road
Cos Cob, CT 06807-2514
http://www.teachersource.com

Fisher Science Education
485 S. Frontage Road
Burr Ridge, IL 60521
(800) 955-1177
http://www.fisheredu.com/

Frey Scientific
100 Paragon Parkway
Mansfield, OH 44903
(800) 225-3739

Nasco-Fort Atkinson
P.O. Box 901
Fort Atkinson, WI 53538-0901
(800) 558-9595

Nasco-Modesto
P.O. Box 3837
Modesto, CA 95352-3837
(800) 558-9595
http://www.nascofa.com

Sargent-Welch/VWR Scientific
P.O. Box 5229
Buffalo Grove, IL 60089-5229
(800) SAR-GENT
http://www.SargentWelch.com

Science Kit & Boreal Laboratories
777 East Park Drive
Tonawanda, NY 14150
(800) 828-7777
http://sciencekit.com

Ward's Natural Science Establishment
P.O. Box 92912
Rochester, NY 14692-9012
(800) 962-2660
http://www.wardsci.com

Glossary

aorta—The body's largest artery. It carries oxygenated blood from the heart's left ventricle to all other arteries except the pulmonary artery.

aortic valve—A valve between the heart and the aorta that allows blood to flow into the aorta but prevents it from flowing back into the heart.

appendicular skeleton—The parts of the skeleton that attach to the axial skeleton. It includes arms, legs, scapula, clavicle, and pelvis.

artery—An elastic, muscular-walled vessel that carries blood away from the heart.

atria—The two (right and left) thin-walled upper chambers of the heart.

autonomic nervous system—The part of the nervous system that controls unconscious actions, such as heart beats and breathing.

axial skeleton—The central part of the skeleton consisting of the skull, vertebrae, ribs, and sternum.

bicuspid valve—See *mitral valve*.

bone marrow—Fatty tissue in bone cavities. Marrow may be red or yellow. Red bone marrow makes red blood cells.

brain stem—The lower side of the brain where centers for involuntary actions such as heartbeat and breathing are located.

capillaries—The tiny blood vessels that connect the smallest arteries with the smallest veins.

cardiac muscle—Muscle tissue found only in the heart. Its fibers have striations, but they are less distinct than those in skeletal muscle, and the cells are smaller.

carpals—The eight small bones of the wrist.

cartilage—A tough, fibrous connective tissue. Also called gristle.

central nervous system—The brain and spinal cord.

cerebellum—A region of the brain concerned with balance and fine movement control. It is located behind the brain stem.

cerebrum—The largest part of the brain. It has two sides, or hemispheres, and contains the centers for thought, sensations, and voluntary movements.

cervical vertebrae—The seven vertebrae found in the neck.

clavicle—A bone that extends sideways on both sides of the top of the chest and connects with the sternum, or breastbone. Commonly called the collarbone.

coccygeal vertebrae—The four vertebrae at the very end of the backbone. The bones are fused to one another and to the pelvis. The fused coccygeal vertebrae are called the coccyx. In many animals the coccygeal vertebrae, which lie in the animal's tail, are separate and more numerous.

cornea—The transparent spherical covering at the front of the eyeball.

diaphragm—The sheet of muscular tissue that separates the chest from the abdomen.

diastole—The time during which the heart is relaxing and blood pressure is at a minimum.

digestive system—The long tube consisting of mouth, pharynx, esophagus, stomach, small intestine, and large intestine, as well as associated organs, which include the liver, gall bladder, and pancreas, that breaks down food, absorbs nutrients, and filters waste.

enzyme—A protein that speeds up (catalyzes) chemical reactions.

epidermis—The outer layer of the skin.

epithelium—Thin tissue, often a single layer of cells, that covers internal organs and the outer surface of the body.

femur—The upper leg bone. The rounded head at its upper end fits into a concavity in the pubis.

fibula—The smaller of the two bones in the lower leg; lies on the outer (lateral) side of the leg.

hair follicle—A pit in the surface of the skin where a single hair grows.

hemoglobin—The protein in red blood cells that combines with oxygen.

hormone—A chemical released into the bloodstream by an endocrine gland.

humerus—The upper arm bone.

hypothalamus—A small organ at the base of the brain where the nervous and endocrine systems interact.

ilium—The bone on either side of the pelvis that you can feel on each side of your hips.

ischium—The pelvic bone, one on each side, that you sit on.

joints—The points about which your bones move relative to one another.

ligaments—The tissues that connect and hold bones together.

lumbar vertebrae—The five vertebrae found in the lower back.

mandible—The lower jawbone; the only major movable bone in the human skull.

metacarpals—The five bones in the back of your hand. Their lower ends articulate with the phalanges, or fingers; their upper ends articulate with the carpals.

metatarsals—The bones that lie between the toes (phalanges) and the ankle (tarsals). They correspond to the metacarpals in the hand.

mitral valve—The valve that lies between the atrium and ventricle on the left side of the heart. Also called the bicuspid valve.

motor neuron—A nerve cell that transmits nerve impulses to muscles.

muscle's insertion—The place where one end of a voluntary muscle is attached to a bone that moves when the muscle contracts.

muscle's origin—The place where one end of a voluntary muscle is attached to a bone that remains relatively fixed.

neuron—A single nerve cell.

nonstriated muscles—Smooth muscles. Also known as involuntary muscles because they cannot be consciously controlled.

parasympathetic nervous system—One division of the autonomic nervous system. It conserves the body's energy by, for example, decreasing the heart rate.

patella—The kneecap.

periosteum—A tough, protective tissue covering all bone surfaces except joints. It contains blood vessels and nerve cells and can form new bone cells.

phalanges—The small bones that make up the fingers of each hand and the toes of each foot.

pubis—Pelvic bones that join to form the front of the pelvis at the lowest part of the abdomen. You can feel them on either side of your body at the base of your groin.

pulmonary artery—A blood vessel that carries deoxygenated blood from the right ventricle of the heart to the lungs.

pulmonary valve—A valve between the heart and the pulmonary artery that allows blood to flow into the artery but prevents it from flowing back into the heart.

radius—One of the two bones of the lower arm. Its lower end is above the thumb side of the wrist.

sacral vertebrae—Five vertebrae in the lower back that are fused together and are often referred to as the sacrum. They are also fused with the bones of the pelvis.

scapula—A bone that is connected to the clavicle and has a concave depression on its outside, into which the end of the humerus (upper arm bone) fits. Commonly known as the shoulder blade.

spinal cord—The body's major nerve cells that connect the brain with the muscles and sensory cells of the body below the head. It passes through the openings in the many vertebrae that make up the vertebral column, which protects it.

sternum—The bone at the front and center of the chest that extends from the collarbone (clavicle) to the abdomen. Commonly known as the breast bone.

striated muscles—Muscles with microscopic stripes across their cells. Also called voluntary muscles because they are under a person's control.

styloid process—See *ulna.*

sympathetic nervous system—A division of the autonomic nervous system that prepares the body to expend energy by, for example, increasing the heart rate.

tarsals—The seven bones of the ankle.

tendons—The tissues that connect muscles to bones.

thoracic vertebrae—The twelve vertebrae found at the back of the chest.

tibia—The shinbone, the larger of the two bones of the lower leg.

tricuspid valve—The valve that lies between atrium and ventricle on the right side of the heart.

ulna—One of the two bones of the lower arm. Its upper end is the elbow; its lower end is the knobby styloid process above the little-finger side of the wrist.

ureters—Tubes that carry urine from the kidneys to the bladder.

urethra—Tube through which urine passes from the bladder to outside the body.

vena cava—Any of the large veins that carries blood to the right atrium of the heart. The inferior vena cava carries blood from the lower parts of the body, and the superior vena cava carries blood from the upper part of the body.

ventricles—Two thick-walled chambers of the heart (right and left) that pump blood into the aorta and the pulmonary artery.

vertebra—One of the bones of the vertebral column.

vertebral column—The numerous bones (vertebrae) that make up the backbone. These bones enclose and protect the spinal cord.

xiphoid process—The pointed bony part of the lower end of the sternum.

Further Reading

ABC's of the Human Body. Pleasantville, N.Y.: Reader's Association, Inc., 1987.

Gardner, Robert. *Crime Lab 101.* New York: Walker, 1992.

———. *Science Projects About the Human Body.* Hillside, N.J.: Enslow Publishers, Inc., 1993.

———. *Health Science Projects About Your Senses.* Berkeley Heights, N.J.: Enslow Publishers, Inc., 2001.

———. *Health Science Projects About Nutrition.* Berkeley Heights, N.J.: Enslow Publishers, Inc., 2001.

The Human Body: An Illustrated Guide to Its Structure, Function, and Disorders. Charles Clayman M.D., editor-in-chief. New York: DK Publishing, 1995.

Swanson, Diane. *Animals Eat the Weirdest Things.* New York: Henry Holt, 1998.

Van Cleave, Janice. *The Human Body for Every Kid.* New York: John Wiley & Sons, 1995.

Internet Addresses

Carnegie Library of Pittsburgh. *Health: Human Anatomy/Physiology.* © 1996–2000. <http://trfn.clpgh.org/hw/health.html>.

CyberFair. *Welcome to CyberFair, The Virtual Science Fair.* March 25, 1998. <http://www.isd77.k12.mn.us/resources/cf/>.

Dennis, L. *Cyberspace Middle School.* "CMS Science Fair Page." © 1996, 1997. <http://www.scri.fus.edu/~cms/>.

The Exploratorium. *The Science Explorer.* © 1998. <http://www.exploratorium.edu/science_explorer/>.

Inner Learning Online. *Human Anatomy Online.* © 1999–2000. <http://www.innerbody.com/htm/body.html>.

Loyola University Chicago, Stritch School of Medicine. *Loyola University Medical Education Network, Master Muscle List.* © 1996–1998. <http://www.lumen.luc.edu/lumen/meded/grossanatomy/dissector/mml/index.htm>.

SciFair.org and John W. Gudenas, Ph.D. *The Ulti3mate Science Fair Resource.* <http://www.scifair.org>.

Index

muscles, 31–51
    all-or-none law, 32
    as levers, 42–46
    chicken wing, 47–48
    fatigue, 39, 41–42
    major, diagram of, 34
    nonstriated (smooth, involuntary), 32
    origins and insertions, 32
    paired, 35, 38
    striated (voluntary), 31–32

N

nervous system, 96–99
    and reaction time, 105–107
    and reflexes, 102–104

O

opposable thumb, 40

P

pectoralis, 36
pelvis, 22–23
phalanges, 21
pulse, 58–59

R

radius, 21
residual air, 72–73
respiration, 52
ribs, 22

S

salivation, 90–91

scapula, 20
skeleton, 15–30
    appendicular, 15
    axial, 15
skin, 11
skull, 19–20
sphygmomanometer, 63
sternum, 20
supplemental air, 72–73
swallowing, 88–89
    and gravity, 88
    sounds, 89
sweat and body temperature, 13

T

teeth, 83–87
    deciduous and permanent, 85–87
tidal air, 72–73
tissue, 11
triceps brachii, 35

U

ulna, 20
urine
    testing of, 95
    volume, 94–95

V

valves in veins, 65–66
vertebrae, 22
vital capacity, 73–75